PRAISE FOR THE ART OF SERVANT LEADERSHIP

This book is for anyone who feels powerless or trapped by his or her corporate culture. Yes, change is possible, and yes, you are the one called to be the change agent! Tony Baron combines elements of psychology, economics, and ministry with the powerful case study of Datron World Communications to bring to life how each of us has the power to transform our organizations via servant leadership. The story of how Art Barter resolved to base his company's leadership principles on what Jesus taught and did is both an inspiration and a blueprint for taking the plunge. This book is not about setting up window-dressing programs to pretend to be doing good. It is about being willing to undertake the toughest leadership challenge of all—to transform oneself to truly serve others.

MARK GARDNER, VICE PRESIDENT AND GENERAL MANAGER
ADVANCED GENOMIC SYSTEMS, LIFE TECHNOLOGIES, INC.

An engaging and uplifting book! W̲ ̲ ̲ ̲ ̲ ews to hear that companies can care about peo̲ ̲ ̲ ̲ ̲ fit! The story of Datron's transformatio ̲ ̲ ̲ ̲ ̲ ̲o late for bad companies to transform ̲ ̲ ̲ ̲ ̲hip principles. These principles are defin̲ ̲ ̲ ̲ ̲ ̲ ̲..ip. This book should be read by all seekers of be ̲ ̲ ̲ ̲..ip. The path of servant leadership is *the* way that work should ̲ e.

CHRIS G. MATTHEWS, PhD
MOLECULAR IMAGING TECHNOLOGY CONSULTANT

Every young leader in America—in business, nonprofit, politics, education, or religion—should read *The Art of Servant Leadership*. It is strong, healing medicine for everyone who has lost faith in the possibility of leadership that is simultaneously ethical and effective. Tony Baron not only shows *what* is achievable through servant leadership, but he also tells us a story of *how,* based on the leadership of Art Barter, CEO of Datron.

Dr. Todd Hunter
Adjunct Professor of Leadership
Pastor, Holy Trinity Church, Costa Mesa, CA
Bishop, Anglican Mission in the Americas

Leadership is a choice and a practice. Tony Baron's life practice of observing and living servant leadership is richly portrayed in *The Art of Servant Leadership* and will help all who read it to step into their power as servant leaders. During my thirty years of teaching leadership in organizations, I have interacted with thousands of individuals looking for a way to become the leader they sought to be when they took on a leadership position. They are committed yet often distracted and even derailed by day-to-day organizational needs and poor role models. Senior leaders who want all to be leaders may not be leveraging their role to model the language, beliefs, and behaviors needed to legitimize and encourage all to be servant leaders. Tony's book, illustrating servant leaders in action, is filled with powerful examples and lessons for all leaders seeking to create a "serving" environment that energizes people to rise to the challenge of meeting the complex needs of their community. I highly recommend you read it.

Victoria Halsey, PhD
VP, Applied Learning
The Ken Blanchard Companies
Author, *The Hamster Revolution*

No one can speak more authoritatively to the subject of leadership and servanthood than Tony Baron. I have worked with Tony personally and he is a servant leader without question. With narcissistic leadership at an epidemic level in the church, nothing could be more timely. This book is destined to become a classic.

Mark Foreman, PhD
Pastor and Author, *Wholly Jesus*

I come from the health care industry, whose sole purpose is to develop technology that is designed for the sake of others' benefit, yet in the end, quarterly driven financial results are what matter. This book is a dynamic and revolutionary systematic approach to organizational leadership that is significant, powerful, and yet still practical to implement. There are many morally founded theoretical leadership models out there, but none convey the sustainability of success that Tony describes here in *The Art of Servant Leadership* as applied at Datron, because it encompasses everyone, from the shipping department to CEO, and every aspect of them as people. I've read many books about integrating Christian values into corporate life but never into the culture of the secular business world as completely and without any religious agenda as found here. Clearly, anyone running a business who wants to operate with a true moral compass has been given a legitimate and proven practical transformational toolkit with *The Art of Servant Leadership* to apply and see the fruit of their labor.

ALEX HAMLOW
FORTUNE 100 HEALTH CARE EXECUTIVE

Dr. Tony Baron quite literally gets to the heart of what matters most in leadership and delivers an inspirational and instructional message on our ability to transform ourselves, our colleagues, the world of business, and the greater global community through living a life of servant leadership.

JENNIFER JUHL
HUMAN RESOURCES EXECUTIVE
FORTUNE 500 DEFENSE INDUSTRY

Dr. Baron does an excellent job in connecting principle with practical example in this thorough guide through servant leadership. If you want to get a different perspective on leading a business and serving people, this is a must-read.

JEREMIE KUBICEK
CEO OF GiANT IMPACT AND
CO-FOUNDER OF THE GiANT COMPANIES

In an era where headlines are full of corporate greed, CEOs' abuse of power, and corruption in leadership, the story of Art Barter and Datron World Communications renews hope and faith that success can be achieved through sacrifice and service for the sake of others. Datron's growth under such leadership is truly inspirational. Tony Baron has produced a road map for corporate success. This book is a must-read for all leaders who believe in the dignity and value of those who work in their organizations.

JAIMEE PITTMAN
PRINCIPAL AND CEO
BARON CENTER, INC.

Some approaches to servant leadership read more like leadership abdication. This is especially the case in relation to leadership in church and other nonprofit institutions, which are heavily reliant on volunteers. Tony Baron cuts through such misunderstandings by applying the biblical concept of servant leadership to the business world, in which healthy, vibrant leadership must be exercised for a company to thrive in the marketplace. He roots the principles of servant leadership in specific case study, which provides both credibility and insight. He demonstrates that servant leadership is self-effacing and entails the empowering of others. Applied to the not-for-profit sector, it means that the servant leader is prepared to do anything but refuses to be pressured into doing everything. There is all the difference in the world between wearing a towel and becoming a doormat.

DR. EDDIE GIBBS
AUTHOR, *LEADERSHIPNEXT: CHANGING LEADERS IN A CHANGING CULTURE*
SENIOR PROFESSOR, FULLER THEOLOGICAL SEMINARY

The Art of Servant Leadership has been perfectly mastered by only one, and Jesus was only able to employ it for about three years. Tony Baron's superbly structured treatise enables individuals to read—and inwardly digest—the essentials of how to become artists of servant leadership. His logical approach of taking failure of contemporary leadership and fixing it by providing the steps to becoming a new kind of leader, a servant leader, is the true essence leading to the formula for success "for the sake of others." This book, with its illuminating examples, should most certainly become standard reading for individuals, corporate and governmental managers, as well as military officers.

RICHARD LYON
REAR ADMIRAL, SEAL
U.S. NAVY (RETIRED)

Leadership never exists in a vacuum. It only truly manifests on the ground, with real people in real situations. Tony Baron, in this book, offers a compelling case study of leadership in action, leadership tested by adversity. This book provides an important perspective on leadership. Not only is leadership seen in the midst of real struggle, but more leadership is presented as something that emerges from the heart and core values of the leader. The primary metaphor of turning the process upside-down, but actually right-side-up is that of a servant. The driving passion "for the sake of others" infuses the leadership task with an energy that is sustainable and brings transformative change. Read this book and see how this model of leadership and influence is lived out in real life.

KURT N. FREDRICKSON, PhD
ASSOCIATE DEAN FOR DOCTOR OF MINISTRY
AND CONTINUING EDUCATION, ASSISTANT PROFESSOR
OF PASTORAL MINISTRY, FULLER THEOLOGICAL SEMINARY

It's the last Friday of the quarter, you're avoiding going to work, the pressure is mounting with each passing minute, you're anxious, tired, stressed, and wondering how you're going to spin the story to corporate when the profit and loss misses the mark … have you ever been there in your career? Who hasn't? What if you could change all that? What if you could change the paradigm that grips so many companies and so many valuable employees working for them? Well, you can! In this brilliant book, *The Art of Servant Leadership: Designing Your Organization for the Sake of Others,* Dr. Tony Baron walks you through how you can profoundly propel your company, your employees, and your life to greatness. With true-life examples and questions for reflection and discussion, this inspiring story of the servant leaders at Datron and their cultural transformation is a must-read for anyone serious about continuous improvement and living your lives the way you were meant to lead. Your heart, your calling, your gifts, and your impact on the lives of others will forever be a source of inspiration and encouragement for those who dare to become servant leaders. This book and its profound truths can lead you down this path with confidence, character, and clarity of purpose.

KEVIN SUMSTINE, PRESIDENT, WHAT BOX

The Art of Servant Leadership

Designing Your Organization for the Sake of Others

Tony Baron, PhD

God bless you!

Tony Baron

Mark 10:45

The Art of Servant Leadership: Designing Your Organization for the Sake of Others

Published by Wheatmark®
610 East Delano Street, Suite 104
Tucson, Arizona 85705 U.S.A.
www.wheatmark.com

International Standard Book Number: 978-1-60494-390-0 (paperback)
Library of Congress Control Number: 2009941899 (paperback)
International Standard Book Number: 978-1-60494-423-5 (hardcover)
Library of Congress Control Number: 2010921547 (hardcover)

To Art and Lori Barter

True Servant Leaders

Contents

Part 1: THE NEED FOR A NEW KIND OF LEADER

   - Titan and Datron: A Difficult Marriage
   - What Went Wrong?
   - The Price of Power
   - Power with a Moral Imperative
   - The Personality of True Power
   - The Pain of Power: Corporate Chronic Stress Syndrome
   - Table Talk

   - The Impact of Great Models
   - Defining Moments Create a New Kind of Leader
   - Servant Leaders See Their Defining Moments as Sacred
   - Servant Leaders Seize Their Defining Moments
   - Servant Leaders Use Their Defining Moments to Clarify Their Values

Contents

Contents

Contents

Foreword

Tony Baron and I met in late 2004, when I was looking for a consulting company to assist with the development of our company mission, purpose, and values. Within ten minutes of our first meeting, we ended up in prayer together. God brought us together for reasons that were beyond our own understanding at the time. Tony has been my mentor, spiritual advisor, accountability partner, and a great friend. He has helped me understand what obedience looks like and how to apply it in my everyday life, and he has helped me in my own servant leader transformation.

I believe Tony Baron has captured the heart of Datron in this book and provides a great argument for why leaders today are so far off course. He challenges leaders to create organizations for the sake of others, not just for profits. The power appetite of leaders today, ones that are self-serving, is leading to the demise of our great nation, of great companies, and great individuals. It is sad to witness those who have such an influence over others choose the path of self first and everyone else later. Some have ended up in confinement, while others have lost everything they owned or those they love.

Leaders, those that have influence over others, should read what Tony has to say about how power today is misapplied. From the family to the boardroom to the manufacturing floor, we have all seen damage done by self-serving leaders who misapply the power they have been given. Leaders need to understand the culture they create through their words and actions and the climate they set by their inconsistent behavior—and especially the impact they have on those around them.

Leaders at Datron have been going through their transformation for several years now. Some have shown great progress; some are lagging behind. Remember, we all go through this transformation at a different pace, and what is easy for some is difficult for others. Embrace and respect that difference, learn to work as a team with those differences, and as John Maxwell states in his book about dreams, "it will take you longer to convince people of where your heart is. It will require patience on your part. And waiting until people engage at the heart level isn't a sign of weakness. It's a sign of wisdom. Strength lies not in streaking ahead but in adapting one's stride to the slower pace of others while continuing to lead. If we run too far ahead, we lose our power of influence."[1]

Transformation to servant leadership is a lifelong process. It is not something you read about one weekend and check off the box on Monday that you've arrived and are now a servant leader.

I love to tell jokes and stories. I use them at meetings with other leaders to illustrate what I am trying to teach or inspire. I really love the stories you will read later in this book about several employees at Datron. They touch my heart deeply and provide confirmation that we are working within the gifts God gave us all for the sake of others.

I would suggest you start a file called the "This is why I do what I do" file. This file will be used to hold thank you notes, bless you notes or e-mails, letters from those you've impacted, and stories you will hear from your employees. This is your file of confirmations that your transformation into servant leadership is working. If you live your life, design your company for the sake of others, and teach those you influence the same, your file will be overflowing.

Tony Baron has impacted my life deeply. He has a great servant's heart, and we are fortunate to have him as the president of our Servant

Foreword

Leadership Institute. I would encourage you to take what he shows you in this book and put it to work in your life at home and at your place of employment. It will be a life-changing experience, all for the sake of others.

ART BARTER

PRESIDENT AND CEO

DATRON WORLD COMMUNICATIONS, INC.

Acknowledgments

It is in silence that the delicate relationship between writer and words comes alive. But a book is never formed alone. It takes a village of committed friends, family, and colleagues to shape the thoughts you are now reading.

Bobbi, thank you for believing in me, encouraging me, and making me laugh. Thank you for reading all the drafts and providing me with honest feedback. I love my life with you. I am blessed to be your husband and partner in ministry. As the years seem to go by faster and faster, you are still the most beautiful person I have ever seen. I love you, Babe!

Sheri, words fail me in expressing my gratitude to you for examining the manuscript in detail and providing me with extensive comments. I deeply appreciated your consistent encouragement that this book was worth writing, along with your important challenges to clarify and make relevant the important concepts of servant leadership. You are a true servant leader who has made a significant mark in my life. Thank you for your commitment to excellence.

Thank you to the Baron Center team. Jeanne, thank you for creating the table talks for each chapter. I love your heart for people and your skill in developing curriculum for training future servant leaders. Your spirit of cooperation inspires me. Michael, thank you for demonstrating servant leadership by your words and your life to the Datron team. Your

Acknowledgments

skills as a trainer and executive coach are marvelous. Folks will be reading your books in the future. And Pitt, thank you for taking what Bobbi and I gave you at BCI and making it better. You have a great team, and you are a great person. It has always been an honor to call you my friend.

Thank you to the servant leadership team. Kathy, you are a wonderful teammate. As an author yourself, you know how difficult it is to move from paragraph to paragraph, chapter to chapter. Thank you for all your support. Skip, Ligaya, Brian, Mark, and Gary all play vital roles as executives within Datron World Communications and within the Servant Leadership Institute. Thank you for being part of this important steering committee so that Datron can serve as a model for others to see that organizations can profitably exist while ultimately meeting the needs of others.

Thank you to Fred, Bruno, and John for providing the inspiring examples of servant leadership at home and abroad. Thank you to the employees of Datron. Since I have been part of this family, I have been deeply touched by your commitment to the principles of servant leadership and your care for one another—thank you.

Thank you to my faith community at St. Anne's. Bobbi and I have been enriched by your faith, hope, and love. Serving as your priest and pastor the last seven and a half years only made our hearts enlarge, our minds expand, and our thinking about the world more engaging. My transition from corporate to church, and now, to a dual ministry of serving churches and corporations worldwide makes me grateful to God for the privilege of being your shepherd.

I want to thank several bishops within the worldwide Anglican Communion that have seeded my thinking and encouraged me along the way. Thank you, to Bishop Todd Hunter, for coining the phrase "for the sake of others" in reference to his new church planting movement in the United States. Todd provided the personal epiphany that expanded my thinking that all of life, institutional and incarnational, secular and sacred, exists for the sake of others. Todd is a great friend and a great servant leader committed to extending God's vision to God's people for a world that God loves. Thank you, Todd. Thank you also to Bishop Frank Lyons for being a support to Bobbi and me during this process of writing. Your encouragement to obey the calling made my transition from St. Anne's to the Servant Leadership Institute easier—thank you, Frank.

And last, but not least, my deepest appreciation to my dear friend Art Barter. When we first met, you had just become the owner of this small, $10 million communications company. In four short years, the company has grown tenfold and continues to grow. Art, you have provided me the opportunity to write again, think more deeply on how we can make a difference in the world, and communicate these universal, timeless truths on servant leadership to those on domestic and foreign soil. I have been enriched by your friendship and your servant leadership. Thank you for believing in this project and the projects to come so that organizations of all brands can learn to live out their purpose for the sake of others. Like you, I am committed to making this world a better place. Thank you!

Servant Leadership—
To equip, inspire, and encourage those we influence in order to make a
profound positive difference in the world

Introduction

The measure of a man is what he does with power.
—PITTACUS

Leaders come in all sizes and from all places. They can be male or female, elderly or youthful, dynamic or reserved. They can come from the elite Ivy Leagues or from the streets of East Los Angeles. Leaders can speak with a heavy accent or be as refreshingly clear as a glass of iced tea on a hot, summer day. But all effective leaders have at least four things in common: vision, values, purpose, and the ability to attract followers.

This book is about one leader with those four qualities: Art Barter.

The Art of Servant Leadership is not intended to be a biographical sketch of this man, but a case study of the principles and practices Art Barter used as a servant leader to reform Datron and transform lives inside and outside the company. There is no question that Art Barter is a man of faith, but even more importantly, he is a faithful man who refuses to let obstacles get in the way of the opportunities to make a profound difference in the lives of others.

Just as leaders come in all sizes and from all places, so do followers. You will read about them within these pages. They are the real heroes, who believed that personal convictions, public responsibilities, and private enterprises like Datron could be integrated to make this world a better place. The accomplished executive team was willing to forsake

Introduction

personal ambitions and past practices of management in order to unite under the banner of servant leadership. Like all of us, they have stumbled and struggled in trying something new and different, yet the fruit of their labor provided models for others to see that they were truly committed to these principles.

With all the books on leadership, what are the distinctive marks that make this book different and worth reading? First, this book offers a case study of an actual business undergoing a transformation to servant leadership. Within the case study, you will see a step-by-step guide on how to transform your organization into a new way of thinking about profit, efficiency, and dignity within the workplace. Secondly, the end of each chapter contains a very important interactive section entitled Table Talk. You can use these questions for a time of personal reflection or have these important conversations in a department meeting or even at a corporate retreat. Thirdly, this book can be used as a training manual within your organization. Each chapter outlines an important concept in leadership: power; dealing with defining moments in leadership; overcoming adversity; the importance of self-leadership; creating and cultivating a servant leadership culture; developing vision, values, and virtues within an organization; and how to extend servant leadership principles to make a difference in the world.

This book is divided into two parts. The first part begins by revealing the tyranny of misguided power and the trauma of disengaged people. You will see Datron before servant leadership. It may sound a great deal like the "average" company to you, where the outside of the company looks beautiful but the underbelly reveals a dark and self-serving side.

The rest of the section will change the way you view your business, your people, and yourself. Leaders need to have an epiphany in order to change the way they do business so that their corporate culture can change the way they live life. You will observe the personal story of Art Barter as he transitions from a traditional leader to the new kind of leader needed today. You will learn how to maximize the defining moments in the life of the leader and how adversity becomes the best teacher for a corporate executive interested in developing credibility within the organization.

All through this section, the Datron story will be used as a case study to illustrate the development of a servant leader. I will attempt to expose the roadblocks and speed bumps so that you can avoid them. In the last two chapters of this section, you will see the significant triggering events that led Art Barter to become a servant leader that set in motion the nearly miraculous purchase of Datron World Communications, Inc.

The second section is designed to help you understand the formula for success as a servant leader. The closing chapters will help you incarnate and influence others toward the principles and practices of servant leadership. My goal is that your servant leadership I.Q. will match your I Do! Most leaders have the intellectual insight to understand the significance of servant leadership. What they lack is the willingness to practice these important principles in light of the stressors, worries, and fears of everyday business. They default to misguided power that deconstructs efficiency and disengages employees to achieve greater goals. My goal is that I want you to be able to equip, inspire, and encourage those whom you influence. Milton Friedman was wrong when he said that the "sole goal of a business is to maximize profit." *I am here to say to all that the sole goal of a business is to exist for the sake of others*. This includes profits, but it also includes all the stakeholders: stockholders, executives, employees, communities, and the well-being of the world.

Great leaders are truly servant leaders. But, you may ask, do they help the bottom line? Research has shown that effective leadership improves the bottom line. According to the work of Jack Zenger and Joseph Folkman,[1] the most effective leaders create five times more profit than poor leaders and twice the amount of profit of an average leader. Truly, this kind of leadership makes all the difference in the world!

Because each organization is unique, with differing histories and distinctive products, I will show you (based on our experience) the universal principles of servant leadership that will work, if implemented correctly, regardless of size or type of organization. Servant leadership is not designed to be a program. Instead, it's a learned process for looking at people and business plans in a new and distinctive way. In these pages you will observe our indebtedness to several organizational leaders and their writings, for they helped Datron, Art Barter, and me to provide clarity to this community.

One final comment: Over the years, I have authored or coauthored four other books as a behavioral scientist and organizational specialist. Through speaking and consulting, I have had the opportunity to work with most of the Fortune 100 companies in the last twenty years. My work has always brought me a great deal of satisfaction, knowing that I am helping people to be better or to get better. Yet, in all my experience, I have never experienced the teamwork and the commitment toward servant leadership as I have at Datron. In the course of this book, you will read the words of Art Barter and hear the testimonies of the many servant leaders that represent Datron. It is in that spirit that I must use the word "we."

Part 1

THE NEED FOR A NEW KIND OF LEADER

1

Leadership and Misguided Power

The Powers are good.
The Powers are fallen.
The Powers must be redeemed.

—WALTER WINK

1997 was a significant year in power gained, lost, and transferred. Bill Clinton began his second term as president of our country. China resumed control of Hong Kong, ending 156 years of British rule. Diana, Princess of Wales, was killed in a car accident. The Nobel Prize winner and humanitarian, Mother Teresa, passed away.

Half a world away, John J. DiGioia, president of Datron World Communications, Inc., was recognizing the talent of his new vice president of finance. Hired in October 1997, Art Barter was a quick study in understanding international markets and strategic financing and in securing the right kind of talent necessary for future Datron success.

Datron was located in Escondido (in the northeast corner of San Diego County) near Interstate 15. The campus had four unattached buildings, each operating as a silo from the other. Even in laid-back Southern California, coats and ties were highly encouraged. Like most public companies, this small corporation was driven by quarterly earnings. The insiders, known for their longevity with the president, often looked at their staff and employees as tools to be utilized to achieve the financial goals of the organization. According to one staff member, there was mutual distrust between the general manager and the head of operations.

Art Barter didn't really know any better. In fact, the only time Art really experienced a difference was at Disneyland, while he was working his way through college. Most of his other experiences reinforced his training that companies are simply about making money. Employees are hired to "make money, save money, increase production, or cut costs." The leadership style was viewed as traditional and authoritative, where titles were critical and office locations were significant. Art understood the game. In fact, he was very successful in playing the corporate competition challenge. He liked the products and he loved creating new international clients, especially when people said it couldn't be done.

Based on his performance, Art soon became the vice president of finance and operations. The culture within Datron was heavy on temporary employees, which made it difficult to increase company loyalty. The employee turnover rate was higher than most companies in the area. A significant activist shareholder group was putting pressure on Datron World Communications's parent corporation, Datron Systems, to change the board in hopes of increasing shareholder profits. By the year 2000, Datron had moved to nearby Vista, California, with an additional facility in Simi Valley near Los Angeles.

During this same period, farther south in San Diego, Gene Ray, with a doctorate in theoretical physics from the University of Tennessee, was leading a very successful company that created new technologies in an effort to launch innovative businesses that specialized in broadband telecommunications. He cofounded the company in 1981, leaving Science Applications International Corporation after losing an argument with his boss. His new company was called The Titan Corporation. Within two weeks, Gene Ray landed a $560,000 contract to design a communication system for GTE. At its height, Titan had eleven thousand employees, earned $1.6 billion in revenue and experienced 30 percent annual growth.[1]

TITAN AND DATRON: A DIFFICULT MARRIAGE

By 2001, Titan was quickly becoming an acquisition machine. On August 6, 2001, Titan purchased 71 percent of Datron Systems stock for $51 million. Titan believed Datron was a good strategic fit since they made satellite tracking antennas and produced voice and data communications products. Many voices within Titan and Datron spoke of a long-term relationship and no significant changes in staff reduction during the purchase negotiations. However, not all the leadership voices were unified. According to Eric DeMarco, then Titan's chief operating officer, there was "obviously a strong potential to consolidate facilities."[2]

Distrust is an awful feeling, one that causes negative consequences. When individuals doubt the integrity of one another, and are highly suspicious of each other's motives, a quality mutual relationship is impossible. Since corporations are composed of individuals, the systems of distrust within a company produce a disease that is destructive to profitability, efficiency, and employee dignity.

The old Datron struggled with trust issues that produced greater delays and higher costs in product development. The pressure to book new business increased, and when that failed, executive expectations were set even higher. The marriage was failing. Hope turned to distrust and distrust turned to dysfunction. When Datron could not meet the demands, discussions focused on explanations that "would allow us time to fix the problems."

Nothing really changed, except the stakes became higher. Still driven by quarterly results, the leadership became more authoritative and demanding to the workforce. Something very ugly was taking place within the company. The employees felt the impact, becoming more disengaged with the product and with the process necessary to make a successful business.

WHAT WENT WRONG?

There are almost as many definitions of leadership as there are people who have attempted to define the idea. Reading just some of the famous definitions shows you how elusive it can be:

- "A leader is a dealer in hope." Napoleon Bonaparte[3]

- "A leader takes people where they want to go. A great leader takes people where they don't necessarily want to go, but ought to be." Rosalynn Carter[4]

- "Leadership is the art of influencing and directing people in such a way that will win their obedience, confidence, respect, and loyal cooperation in achieving common objectives." U.S. Air Force[5]

- "Leadership is the process of influence." Ken Blanchard[6]

The one common concept that all these definitions acknowledge is that leadership is *applied power*. This kind of leadership can be used by power brokers for good or for harm, for one or for many. For example, Genghis Khan, the ruthless Mongolian leader and murderer of thousands, would fit the description. So would the terrorist Osama Bin Laden, the military conqueror Alexander the Great, or even the former chairman of NASDAQ, Bernard Madoff, guilty of the largest investor fraud ever committed by a single person.[7] The same description could be used of positive social change agents like Martin Luther King, Jr., Mahatma Gandhi, or even Mother Teresa. But the best leaders understand the moral imperative within leadership. They know that leadership can never be morally neutral.

If leadership is simply applied power without a moral imperative, then leaders are often led by their own devices to determine what is really important within a company. Usually, this is the desire for profitability. Unfortunately, when the main purpose (in some cases the only purpose) of companies is profitability, the result is employees that are sacrificial pawns on the chessboards of powerful corporate kings and queens. The only stakeholders of consequence are the shareholders. Sadly, the employees, customers, society, and the organization itself are poorer for it. So a good company, with aspirations of becoming a great company, falls and fails when it does not have a solid foundation of moral leadership. It fails to make this world a better place, and it fails to lead the individual participants to experience individual and community greatness.

THE PRICE OF POWER

Leaders generally have an aggressive appetite for power. The best legal minds may use it in the courtroom to manipulate jurors. Senators and congressional leaders crave it within the White House. Lobbyists brag about their influence within the District of Columbia beltway. Executives covet it in the boardroom. Managers desire it on the assembly floor. However, the desire for power is not reserved only to the courtroom, capitol buildings, or corporations. You see it everywhere, even on reality television programs. Whether you're a parent or a parish priest, you are faced with the many privileges and perplexities of power. The eminent psychiatrist Paul Tournier, in his masterful work *The Violence Within*, writes, "Power has become the supreme value, the only one that is universally recognized."[8] Our craving for success without significance has made power the modern idolatry of our times.

The most serious problem in leadership today is not the lack of leaders, but the misuse and abuse of applied power. We have many leaders, but they are the wrong kind. The modern world, with its materialistic worldview, sees power as primarily money-oriented. The preindustrial world understood the significance of spiritual factors associated with the concept of power. Today, most psychologists and theologians in our postmodern culture understand the concept of power as the convergence of both spiritual and material.

Any given manifestation of power (individually and institutionally) has spiritual and material dimensions. Every power has an outside face, but every power also has an inward driving force. The outside face can be the institution itself, the chosen leaders of that institution, or even the laws of a territory. The inner essence of power needs the outside face, much like our inner spirit needs our body to be intentional about our desires. They need each other to survive.

If leadership lacks a moral imperative, it becomes an idolatrous exercise that eventually will cause the disengagement of its employees and the death of the organization.

Examples abound even for the casual observer. As mentioned earlier, Bernard Lawrence Madoff founded the Wall Street firm Bernard L. Madoff Investment Securities LLC in 1960 and was the chairman of the board until his arrest on December 11, 2008.[9] His asset management firm was a massive Ponzi scheme, with losses totaling over $65 billion for its clients. Once thought of as a great philanthropist, serving on boards of major nonprofit institutions, Madoff is now an inmate at the Metropolitan Correctional Center in New York City serving a maximum sentence of 150 years in prison and owing $170 billion in restitution.[10]

Enron Corporation, one of the world's most renowned energy trading and communications companies, became a symbol of corporate fraud and corruption. Based in Houston, Texas, Enron employed close to 21,000 people at its height in 2001. Starting in 1996 and for five consecutive years thereafter, *Fortune* magazine named Enron "America's Most Innovative Company." In 2000, Enron was listed by that same magazine as one of the "100 Best Companies to Work for in America."

The magazine had no idea how deceived Kenneth Lay, former Enron CFO Andrew Fastow, and their conspirators were as they committed institutional, systematic accounting fraud.[11]

Through a series of scandals, Enron was on the verge of the largest corporate bankruptcy in history. In 2001, the value of investors' equity per share went from $85 to 30 cents. Leadership, in the cases of Madoff and Lay, was the classic story of abuse and misuse of applied power. Whether it was the gullibility of leadership or an innovative attempt to defraud, the American dream for Madoff and Lay turned into an American nightmare.

POWER WITH A MORAL IMPERATIVE

Servant leadership, on the other hand, is power applied with a moral imperative. That imperative is to lead *sacrificially for the sake of others.* The truly great leaders in the world understand that you become more influential when you give your own power away. Great leaders model, equip, inspire, and encourage others toward individual and community greatness. They do not see their colleagues as incompetent or insignificant, but as humans with dignity that they can empower.

Servant leadership is designed to increase the self-determination, self-confidence, and self-sacrifice of everyone. Servant leaders motivate through modeling and proclaiming the importance of service for the sake of others. Giving power away through servant leadership will transform individuals and institutions to become empowered and engaged with the world around them.

THE PERSONALITY OF TRUE POWER

Not one economic expert believes we are living in a period of financial growth. Nearly every business periodical today features primary articles on how to deal with our economic recession. The term "bailout" is heard on Wall Street, in the automotive industry, the banking industry, and in jokes from Jay Leno and David Letterman. The average consumer doesn't know whom to trust or what to believe. People are losing their jobs as well as their confidence in our capitalistic leadership. Why is this happening? Bill George, Harvard University business professor, former chairman and chief executive officer of Medtronic, and author of *True North: Discover Your Authentic Leadership*, believes our economic woes are caused by one reason and one reason only: the failure of leadership.[12]

The failure of leadership is the unwillingness to move beyond material wealth and the willfulness to manipulate people and systems to achieve myopic goals. What is the personality of servant leadership power? In other words, what are the characteristics of applied power, motivated by a moral imperative, to lead sacrificially for the sake of others and the betterment of the world? The answer may be found by looking for three elements that serve as signposts of correctly applied power: creativity, transformation, and redemption.

Creativity

Servant leadership brings order into applied power by breathing life and creativity to all the organization's participants. The importance of creativity for the executive and employee cannot be underestimated or over-appreciated. Creativity suggests imagination, resourcefulness, ingenuity, inventiveness, and vision. The result of creativity is not chaos. In reality, its result is the very opposite: The fruits of creativity bring order, arrangement, prototype, character, understanding, variety, shape, and discipline.

To equip people for creativity is a mark of an effective servant leader. This person knows the significance of endowing power, training leaders, preparing character, and supplying the right kind of information for personal and community success. The very word "creative" comes from our word "creation." Creation is the God-given gift of providing the right conditions where power can operate in harmony with other powers. A servant leader equips for creativity.

Transformation

The second signpost of correctly applied power is the experience of transformation for the leader and for those being led. The role of a servant leader is to stimulate what is already within the person. There are three universal languages in the world: the language of music, the language of love, and the language of dreams. Regardless of birth status or location, every person responds to music, love, and dreams. Over the course of time, their inner wounds, self-inflicted or inflicted by others, make these beautiful languages become distorted, disfigured, and sometimes even muted. Because of their wounds, people are willing to settle for so little in life.

Have you wondered how huge Asian elephants, weighing several tons, are kept in their place by chains around one of their legs staked in the ground at the circus? They have the strength to remove the stakes from the ground but have been conditioned growing up to believe that they cannot remove them. In fact, when the elephants were younger, they didn't have the strength to remove the stakes. They tried, but the stakes were stronger than the smaller elephants. As they grew, they had the strength, but lost the will to remove the barriers because they believed they could not do so.

In the same way, many people have come to wrongly believe that they cannot remove the barriers and obstacles in their lives so that they can achieve their dreams and experience genuine transformation. They have the strength but have lost the will. Psychologists call it learned helplessness. In this book, I call it corporate chronic stress syndrome. You will learn more about this corporate disorder later in this chapter. The point is that servant leaders must provide an environment to stimulate a different kind of thinking that is healthy and whole for the person. He or she must inspire the willingness to change, despite the cost, so the individual can live out their life fully alive.

A genuine transformation redefines levels of competency, character, and chemistry for the people *and* the leader. As James MacGregor Burns, Pulitzer prize winner and author of *Transforming Leadership*, writes, "Transforming leadership ultimately becomes moral in that it raises the level of human conduct and ethical aspiration of both the leader and the led, and thus it has a transforming effect on both."[13] Servant leaders inspire for transformation.

Redemption

Nearly all the leadership books avoid the subject of redemption directly. Why? The term redemption has been used by many in a religious context instead of as a word that refers to a *responsibility*. The Hebrew roots conveying the meaning of redemption, *padah* and *ga'al*, imply the prior existence of an obligation toward another and were originally used in the context of commercial transactions. In the Hebrew scriptures, these two words are applied to a financial redemption of ancestral land from another to whom it has been sold. It is also used to describe a financial redemption of a family member from servitude to another due to debt.[14]

In the investment world, redemption is the return of an investor's principal in a security, such as a stock, bond, or mutual fund. In real estate law, redemption is seen as liberation of an estate in real property from a mortgage. Redemption, therefore, is the act of reclaiming through payment what rightfully belongs to you. Servant leaders encourage redemption through liberation—*the freedom to be responsible in a relationship*. We must persuade, promote, and give confidence to our people that they can take back what rightly belongs to them in the workplace, in particular, responsibility for relationships, dignity of dreams, and efficiency of effort.

THE PAIN OF POWER: CORPORATE CHRONIC STRESS SYNDROME

Power, the true characteristics of power applied with a moral imperative, produces creativity, transformation, and redemption. So what happened at Datron and Enron and in the halls of the capitol buildings? Why did so many people lose the dream and others become unwilling to even try to make a difference? Why were so many people interested in "spinning the story" and only focused on quarterly earnings? I believe it was corporate chronic stress syndrome that led to the misapplication of priorities, the misuse of strategic processes, and the abuse of all the people, including the leaders.

Have you ever noticed that when you are presented with food at your favorite restaurant, you start to salivate? The Russian scientist Ivan Petrovich Pavlov won the 1904 Nobel Prize with his breakthrough research in classical conditioning. He discovered that if a ringing bell or tone is repeatedly paired with the presentation of food to a dog, the dog salivates. Later, all you have to do is ring the bell without the presentation of the food, and the dog will salivate. Yes, just like you do when you read the menu and you haven't been presented the food yet.

In 1965, the American psychologist Martin E. P. Seligman, while studying the relationship between fear and learning, discovered an unexpected phenomenon during experiments on dogs, using classical conditioning. Instead of pairing the tone with food, Seligman paired it with a harmless shock, restraining the three groups of dogs in a harness during the learning phase.[15]

The dogs in Group One were put in the harnesses for a period of time and later released. In Group Two, one dog would be subjected to the electric shock, which the dog could end by pressing a lever. A dog in Group Three was wired in parallel with the dog in Group Two. When the dog in Group Two received an electric shock, the dog in Group Three would receive the same harmless shock. The only difference was that the dog in Group Three could not stop the shock; it had to depend upon the dog in Group Two to touch the lever. To dogs in Group Three, it seemed that the shock ended in random and apparently inescapable timing. The first two groups recovered from the stress of the shocks, but the Group Three dogs in effect learned to be helpless. These dogs exhibited all the symptoms of chronic clinical depression.

The theory of learned helplessness was then extended to human behavior. The conclusion was that what you are thinking determines your behavior. In other words, *outlook determines outcome.* This provided a model for clinicians around the world in explaining more fully the state of depression, primarily their lack of affect and their learning by experience to be helpless. Depressed people, like the dogs in the Group 3 experiment, believe they have no control over their circumstances.

So how does this relate to the business world? Borrowing the ideas of attribution theory from psychology, Seligman discovered that a depressed person thought about the bad event in even more pessimistic ways than a nondepressed person. In fact, three things happened to their thought processes that helped produce a learned helplessness:

- They *personalized* the explanation of their discomfort. They blamed the difficult situation on themselves rather than external factors. For example, they might think "I must be stupid because I can't figure out the solution" or "I must be getting old because this problem is too overwhelming."

- They believed the problem was *pervasive.* The problem they were facing was not just in this particular situation, but the entire company was experiencing the same problem. For example, "No one agrees with this decision" or "Everyone is being treated poorly in this company."

- They believed the problem was *permanent* instead of temporary. They believed that the difficult or uncomfortable situation could not change. They would condemn people by saying to others, "they will not change" or say that the task to complete the project "will never work."

The clinical world seeks to place a diagnosis on the condition. Here, we need to identify the reasons behind the diagnosis.

What are the causes of corporate chronic stress syndrome?

- *Consistent crisis events* usually surrounding quarterly earnings, production goals, and personnel issues. This symptom is usually related to a lack of incarnating critical core values within the organization.

- *Blame orientation and self-promotion* exists within leadership and among departments. There is negligible cooperation as teammates.

- *Abusive language* demonstrates a lack of consistency in treating one another with dignity. Civility is often missing in conduct and conversation.

- *Significant changes in direction* have been made from previous strategic and tactical goals without any justification. The lack of consistent action causes confusion. The inconsistency creates bewilderment and disorientation for the employees.

- *Micromanagement and authoritative style* convey an anxious presence to the employees. The cultural absence of peace stifles creativity and increases corporate anxiety.

- *Employees feel no ownership in the process and believe their suggestions go unheard.* There is little collaboration and a lack of employee empowerment.

- *Leadership views training and development as an expense* instead of an investment. The corporation, under economic and interpersonal stress, eliminates or significantly reduces training opportunities, which results in employees no longer being equipped to fix the present problems.

- *Knowledge is withheld and communication silos* reveal a comprehensive lack of trust within the organization. After all, information is power.

- *Excessive rumors, back-biting, and spinning stories* within the corporate structure convey to all that truth and facts are unimportant.

- *Power struggles and tunnel vision* convince a considerable segment of the workforce to believe that they are simply tools to be used in order to achieve the financial goals of the leadership. The result for the employees is a lack of joy and passion in their labors.

The net business results of corporate chronic stress syndrome are lower efficiency, increased costs, declining innovation, greater conflict, and disengaged people.

Datron, before the implementation of servant leadership, was a classic case of corporate chronic stress syndrome. The executives didn't really have a plan for the future because it didn't really matter. Datron was driven by short-term quarterly earnings. When the quarterly earnings did not meet expectations, corporate chronic stress syndrome spread throughout the organization. It started with the leaders in creating self-serving goals. It was followed by the employees who were disengaged to the purpose, plans, and processes to overcome the obstacles. In truth, everyone felt hopeless to do anything about it.

Despite the obvious obstacles within Datron, the ingredients were still there for success. Art Barter had a mind for numbers and a heart for people. All Art needed was a seasoned professional to teach him about servant leadership to change the direction of Datron. It was an epiphany that changed the course of history for Art Barter and for many others to come.

In conclusion, the crisis in business is simply a crisis in leadership. The world economy demands an alternative way of doing business, and workers demand a different style of leadership. Effective leaders see defining moments as an opportunity to change direction and seek a new destination. Today can be a defining moment for you.

Table Talk

Discussing and Reflecting on Chapter 1

Transformation of a culture to a servant leadership model is a journey that takes time and thought. At the end of each chapter you will find questions to reflect on individually first, and then to use to engage your leadership team in their own personal reflection. Once that is accomplished, set up a series of discussions with the team. Your goal in this first stage of the journey as a leadership team is to describe the current state of your organizational culture.

1. Your Organization's Story

What is your organization's "story"? How did it begin, what phases and changes has it gone through? Who were the leaders? What was their leadership style and focus? How did they use or apply their power? What impact did they have on the beliefs and behaviors of employees?

2. Your Role Models

Who are your leadership role models? In what ways did they use their power? What did you learn from them? How did they shape your beliefs about leadership?

3. Your Leadership Purpose

How would you describe the foundational purpose of your leadership role?

4. Your Assessment

How would you assess your present organizational environment? In each section, check the box that best reflects your present environment.

*A. **Creativity:** Tapping into one's imagination, resourcefulness, ingenuity, inventiveness, and vision.*

❑ People readily share their opinions and ideas and access resources across organizational boundaries in search of continuous improvement of products, processes, and people.

❑ People rarely share innovative ideas for positive change. They defer to their bosses' directives and remain "siloed" in their function/department.

*B. **Transformation:** Committing to continual learning, personal growth and development, and being willing to change beliefs and behaviors in order to serve others and benefit all.*

❑ People are encouraged to continuously grow and develop, readily share information, and feel empowered to make relevant decisions on their own.

❑ People do not perceive their personal growth and development as a priority, are defensive when their beliefs or behaviors are challenged, and are reluctant to openly share information or make decisions on their own.

*C. **Redemption:** Retaining what rightfully belongs to you.*

❑ People are encouraged to express and realize both their personal and professional vision and dreams and to take responsibility for developing trusted relationships that will help them realize those dreams for themselves, their organization, and their community.

❏ People act as if they are helpless and stressed in terms of ever-changing and urgent work priorities. They blame conditions in their life and others as reasons for their inability to effect positive change in their life and at work.

5. Your Summary

In your own words, summarize your thoughts on the present state of your organization's environment.

2

The Leader's Epiphany

*Gratitude bestows reverence, allowing us to encounter everyday epiphanies,
those transcendent moments of awe that change forever how we experience
life and the world.*

—JOHN MILTON

Robert Browning, one of the foremost Victorian poets and playwrights of the nineteenth century, described inspiration as being "stung by the splendour of a sudden thought.¹" There is something wonderful and transforming about a personal epiphany. Those experiences provide opportunities to change our thinking in order to change the direction of our lives.

On May 16, 2004, Art Barter had an epiphany that redefined him as the kind of leader he wanted to be and the kind of person he wanted to become. Art was "stung by the splendour of a sudden thought" that forever changed how he looked at corporate leadership. The container within Art was already filled with all the necessary ingredients, but it took one guest speaker at his church, renowned workplace consultant Ken Blanchard, to convert the ingredients of applied power into leadership modeled after Jesus.

THE IMPACT OF GREAT MODELS

Every leader had a teacher and model. Sometimes they received their education through life experiences with their mentor, and sometimes they received their learning from books. Art Barter was blessed. His mentors included some of the best in the business world and also included the best mentor a boy can ever have: his father. Great models challenge us to greater heights as leaders and great mentors convince us to walk in teachable humility.

Ken Blanchard was Art's first mentor in the art of servant leadership. The key for Art was in the power of the question Ken Blanchard gave at the beginning of his talk. Blanchard asked the thousand-plus attendees to break into small groups and give their definition and description of leadership to one another. After about ten minutes, Blanchard wanted to know by a show of hands how many used the words servant leadership or Jesus in their definition or in their description. In this largely Christian audience, only a dozen were able to raise their hands, and Art Barter was not one of them.

Ken Blanchard built an inspiring case, supported by corporate experiences and biblical references, on the power of servant leadership. He cited Jesus as the definitive role model of servant leadership, and Art began to change his thinking about corporate leadership.

If Blanchard served as an evangelist for Art, then another leadership expert named John Maxwell was his apostle and teacher. A prolific author and trainer, Maxwell has reached more than 15 million people with his leadership concepts. Soon after that eventful evening in May 2004 with Ken Blanchard, Art became acquainted with the *Maxwell Leadership Bible*. This unique study bible was designed to be a resource for those who wanted to learn more about servant leadership.

John Maxwell writes in the introductory section of the bible, "Where do most people go to learn leadership? The answer to that question today is that they search many places. Some examine the world of politics.

Others seek models in the entertainment industry. Many look to the world of business. But the truth is, the best source of leadership teaching today is the same as it has been for thousands of years. If you want to learn leadership, go to the greatest Book on leadership ever written—the Bible."[2] Today, Art Barter is willing to give a *Maxwell Leadership Bible* to anyone at Datron who asks him for one.

These twin towers of leadership expertise, Blanchard and Maxwell, knew the power of servant leadership and they knew Jesus, the person behind these revolutionary teachings. They planted the seeds of servant leadership in Art so that his epiphany could grow and develop. When we look back on Art's life growing up in Southern California, we can see two other ways in which Art was molded for servant leadership.

The first one was by his father's example. Everyone knew Russ Barter was a kind, generous man who had a servant's heart. Before he bought Maloney Tire, a tire and front-end brake shop in Anaheim, California, he worked for twenty years at Pacific Bell. During his free time, one would see Art's dad volunteering at the Kiwanis, Rotary, and the Elks. Russ became president of these chapters by simply practicing servant leadership. People liked to follow Russ, and Art had a great role model in his father.

The second was his work at the Disney Company. Art learned a great deal from working at Disney. Art witnessed their commitment to serving the needs of the public, the establishment of a climate of joy for the employees, and the importance of collaboration in making events memorable. Art credits his dad and the Disney Company for laying the strong foundations and providing the right kind of fertile soil for servant leadership. These early experiences prepared Art to face his future.

DEFINING MOMENTS CREATE A NEW KIND OF LEADER

Let's consider how the people and events in Art's youth became defining moments that enabled Art to develop the necessary skills and right kind of heart to purchase Datron. Leaders view defining moments as divine, providing personal opportunities to change direction and seek a new destination. Such defining moments offer four key principles of servant leadership, detailed below.

SERVANT LEADERS SEE THEIR DEFINING MOMENTS AS SACRED

Most people live their lives unaware of the many defining moments that come and go from their path. One reason, borrowing a phrase from the 1970s progressive English rock band Pink Floyd, is that they have become "Comfortably Numb."[3]

Most people have learned to be comfortably numb. Drugs, drink, entertainment, sports, sex, status, money, and power can serve as their numbing tools in dealing with life. They survive but do not thrive. They are living but not fully alive. They miss the many opportunities to live life fully, often because they don't see life as sacred. Living this kind of life hinders the individual from seeing that life is a series of significant moments designed to define you as a person and a child of God.

Defining moments are designed to provide more than a whisper to us that life is important and that we are significant to our Creator. Servant Leaders may not recognize their defining moments right away, but eventually they will get it. Once they do, they will respect these moments with personal gratitude. Art can testify that his experiences with his dad, the Disney Company, and Maxwell and Blanchard were sacred experiences that defined him and eventually distinguished him from being just another corporate leader.

SERVANT LEADERS SEIZE THEIR DEFINING MOMENTS

No one in the United States will forget September 11, 2001. Within ninety minutes, the most celebrated skyline in the western world collapsed. In less than two hours, thousands of lives were lost, including firefighters, police, and rescue workers trying to help. The city was in shambles, the nation was numb, and one leader among the many leaders of that day knew his *sole* calling was to serve. The defining moment of 9/11 pushed Rudy Giuliani into the limelight of courageous servant leadership.[4] Giuliani summarized his philosophy on leadership with a two-word sign on his city hall desk: I'm Responsible. It was an unwanted role but nevertheless a calling and responsibility that defined him as a leader, statesman, and government servant.

Defining moments propel us forward to serve. Throughout the history of the world, the courageous leaders saw their defining moments not as steps to more status but a calling to serve *sacrificially for the sake of others.* Englishman William Wilberforce's defining moment came when he saw slavery firsthand and devoted the rest of his life as a member of Parliament to end it. Servant leaders do not have to be leaders in government; they can also be a child in the slave labor market within Pakistan. Iqbal Masih was sold to the carpet industry at the age of four, made to work twelve hours a day, and because of insufficient food, barely was able to survive. Iqbal escaped the brutal slavery at the age of ten and joined the Bonded Labor Liberation Front of Pakistan to help stop the cruelty surrounding child labor. Because of his servant's heart, Iqbal helped more than three thousand Pakistani children that were in bonded labor escape to freedom. In 1994 at the age of twelve, he was awarded the Reebok Human Rights Award. One year later, on Easter Sunday in 1995, Iqbal Masih was murdered at the age of thirteen by those opposing his movement. In 2000, Iqbal was posthumously awarded the World's Children's Prize for the Rights of the Child.[5] Even as a child, Iqbal seized his defining moment as a calling to serve sacrificially for the sake of others.

SERVANT LEADERS USE THEIR DEFINING MOMENTS TO CLARIFY THEIR VALUES

All leaders, in particular servant leaders, have an unwavering commitment to their values. In the course of their lives, the defining moments provide opportunities for personal reflection as to what is really important and significant. In essence, they ask, "What am I willing to die for, figuratively and in some cases, literally?" Examples abound of leaders who have had defining moments that led them to sacrifice their lives for their values and attract others as followers to their cause. Abraham Lincoln was assassinated for abolishing slavery in the United States, Nelson Mandela was imprisoned for defending civil rights in South Africa, and Susan B. Anthony was arrested for her efforts to give American women the right to vote.

Of course, one does not have to be famous or sacrifice their life to live out this principle. All leaders, regardless of status, must share this conviction of clarifying values. Leaders must know what they stand for in life, personally and professionally. Defining moments provide the opportunity to clarify your own passionate values. Once clarified, the values can be communicated effectively. Followers believe in the messenger even before they fully understand the implications of the message. In other words, followers must trust the person before they can trust the plan.

Defining moments provide clarity to our values. Leaders' enduring beliefs influence every aspect of their life's journey: morality, relationships, goals, actions, and daily decisions. In a world where the map is constantly changing, values provide us the steady compass to our true north.

SERVANT LEADERS RECOGNIZE THE CONTRIBUTION OF OTHERS

Saying please and thank you are two primary skills our parents taught us growing up. A friend of mine, a retired Anglican bishop, used to tell me that his entire ministry in recruiting volunteers could be summed up by those two phrases: "Please, can you help me?" and "Thank you for working with me!"

Recognition is important, isn't it? Learning to say "thank you" and acknowledging the contribution of others provide fuel for the future. More importantly, recognition increases the opportunities for significantly more defining moments as a group. Synergy is created. Understanding this principle will turn you from a good leader to a great leader.

James Kouzes and Barry Posner, esteemed professors at Santa Clara University, also have studied the powerful effect of recognition upon followers. They believe that recognition must not "be predictable, routine, and impersonal."[6] The element of surprise, the importance of sincerity, and the simplicity of saying "thank you" are important ingredients to motivate others to greater heights professionally and personally. It allows them to have healthy, life-giving, defining moments. The more defining moments there are in the workforce and on the team, the greater the chance that the dream will become a reality for the organization.

We can see this process at work in Art Barter's path to servant leadership. Ken Blanchard and John Maxwell had defining moments in their lives that propelled Art to see the defining moments in his own life. He in turn caused others to have defining moments in their lives.

Because servant leadership is more of an art than a science, it often can be measured through the visceral responses of the followers. Are they motivated? Have these principles changed the way they deal with their family or their marriage? Do they take ownership surrounding production issues? How do they treat one another on the work floor? Does their speech inspire others to greater heights or discourage others? In determining the effectiveness of servant leadership, the ultimate measuring question becomes, "Are we producing other servant leaders?"

Table Talk

Discussing and Reflecting on Chapter 2

1. Your Defining Moments

When you think of your life's story, and how it unfolded, what people, experiences, or events were critical to your development? To recall these defining moments, take a walk through the stages of your life, from early childhood, to adolescence, to young adulthood, to the present moment. You could have experienced these defining moments as either strongly positive or difficult, even negative. Make notes, without judgment, on what thoughts and memories come to mind.

2. Your Personal Epiphanies

What people, experiences, and events impacted your life in ways that changed or clarified your thinking and confirmed the direction of your life? You learned something, you changed and transformed in some way, in your heart and in your mind. In what ways did each of your defining moments shape your thinking, transform you, and influence your life's direction?

3. Your Clarified Values

When you review your defining moments, you can see that these moments helped you clarify your values, those deep-seated guiding principles that have become foundational in your life. What values were clarified or strengthened in the defining moments of your life?

4. Your Revelation

As you look at the life-shaping and life-changing events, you may have the experience that just the right person or the right event occurred at the right time, developing you, giving you choices, moving you forward, even through extreme difficulty. In what ways do you feel you were not alone in the journey of your life and that you were guided through these growth experiences? Do you believe you were and are divinely guided and influenced? Do you view your defining moments as sacred?

5. Your Sources of Leadership Inspiration

What were and are your sources of leadership inspiration? From where do you draw your strength and renew your energy and commitment to lead and teach others? In what ways has your faith become an inspiring guide to you as a leader?

6. Integration of Faith and Work

Do you believe that your faith and your work can be integrated or do you believe they need to be kept separate? How, specifically, do you seek to integrate your faith and your work? How is this reflected in your workplace? In what ways has it impacted your leadership style, your organization's vision, values, and commitment to the people of your organization?

7. Comfort Level with Servant Leadership

In what ways did your defining moments help you learn about leadership as service to others? How would using the term *servant leadership* transform how you think about leadership?

8. Recognizing the Contribution of Others

In what ways do you recognize the contribution of others? Are you paying lip service to recognition or does your recognition come from a genuine belief that the sum is greater than the parts and that the contribution of others increases the depth and breadth of your organization's accomplishments and your personal growth? To what extent would you say the people you lead feel recognized and appreciated by you?

9. Your Assessment

Servant leadership is a continual learning journey. Place a check mark where you believe more reflection or action would be helpful in your journey.

❑ Describing the defining moments of my life.

❑ Acknowledging these defining moments as sacred, divinely influenced.

❑ Recognizing my calling as a leader to serve others.

❑ Knowing my values, the foundational principles that guide my life.

❑ Knowing my sources of leadership inspiration.

❑ Better integrating my faith, my beliefs, and my work.

❑ Increasing my comfort with the term *servant leader*.

❑ Genuinely appreciating and recognizing the contribution of others.

10. Your Summary

Based on this chapter's Table Talk, what next steps will you take to strengthen your commitment to servant leadership?

3

A Servant Leader Is Best
Revealed in Adversity

All the adversity I've had in my life, all my troubles and obstacles, have strengthened me… You may not realize it when it happens, but a kick in the teeth may be the best thing in the world for you.

—Walt Disney

Robert E. Lee knew adversity. General Lee lost his citizenship, his home, his career, his savings, his investments, his daughter, his daughter-in-law, two grandchildren, and countless colleagues in the North and South because of the Civil War.[1] If Lee knew adversity, Abraham Lincoln, recognized by many as the greatest leader the United States ever produced, was the *incarnation* of adversity. Before serving as president in the bloodiest war in our land, Lincoln was fired from a job, failed as a businessman, defeated for state legislature; his sweetheart died of typhoid fever, and he suffered a nervous breakdown all in a period of four years. In the decade before serving as the sixteenth president, he was rejected for land officer, defeated twice for U.S. Senate, and defeated for nomination for the position of vice president. In his personal life, Lincoln's marriage to Mary Todd could best be described as difficult, partly attributed to the death of three of their four sons during their childhood or teenage years. During his presidency, he was ridiculed by the press and mocked by his cabinet.[2] Yes, Abraham Lincoln was the incarnation of adversity. But the sixteenth president of the United States also serves as a model in overcoming failures, life's difficulties, and adverse circumstances.

ADVERSITY INTRODUCES PEOPLE TO THEMSELVES

Adversity has a way of developing previously unknown talents. Adversity also has the power to unleash character flaws or strengths within a leader. Because of the purchase of Datron World Communications, Art will always consider 2004 as a special year. The year ended in triumph, but it started as the greatest trial of his corporate life.

The challenges began because Lockheed Martin Corporation was interested in purchasing Titan, which included Datron World Communications. Lockheed, a military contractor based in Bethesda, Maryland, is the largest contractor in the world to the Pentagon.[3] As a result of the due diligence, an internal investigation was conducted by Lockheed and Titan. Both sides agreed to report their findings to the Department of Justice and the Securities and Exchange Commission. Titan, which had about twelve thousand employees and $2 billion in annual revenue in 2004, had already approved being acquired when the Securities and Exchange Commission made formal allegations against Titan concerning bribery charges in five countries to secure additional business. The charge was that Titan, and in particular, its subsidiary Datron, violated the Foreign Corrupt Practices Act. According to the SEC in their legal complaint filed in the U.S. District Court for the District of Columbia, a senior Titan officer funneled approximately $2 million, via its agent, toward the election campaign of Benin's then-incumbent president. The SEC also alleged that Datron World Communications "paid commissions to local agents in a number of foreign countries that were disproportionately large when compared to Datron's annual revenues."[4]

A Servant Leader Is Best Revealed in Adversity

They alleged that Datron failed to conduct sufficient due diligence in determining whether the unusually high commission payments were really indirect monies paid to foreign officials in violation of the Foreign Corrupt Practices Act. On June 25, 2004, Lockheed terminated the merger agreement. However, the investigation continued.

While Datron's leadership endured public denigration in the press, Art Barter, then vice president of finance, was steadfastly certain that Datron was innocent of all the charges.

During the early stages of the investigation, Art Barter was appointed by Titan to be the general manager of Datron. Art instructed his entire Datron team to fully cooperate with the investigators by sharing any and all information. He divided his senior team into two forces: one ran the company while the other provided the immense amounts of information required by the lawyer-heavy investigation team.

After fifteen months of investigation, Titan consented to a final judgment without admitting or denying the allegations. Datron was not mentioned in any of the charges against Titan for violation of the Foreign Corrupt Practices Act.[5] However, in the current world of mass communication and international media outlets, bad news sticks longer and travels faster than good news. In July 2004, the Titan board of directors voted to retain a broker to attempt to sell Datron World Communications and asked Art Barter to develop a list of potential interested buyers. Art added his name to the bottom of the list.

Because of the bad publicity, most of the potential buyers were not interested in acquiring Datron. The company was doing about $10 million in annual revenue, but its international reputation, in spite of its innocence, took a big hit. The one prospective purchaser who still believed in this company was Art Barter.

The sale of Datron World Communications to Transnortad, a company owned by Art Barter, was officially closed on November 5, 2004. Art had acquired a company with an unfairly damaged reputation that threatened to overshadow its good products. It was just six months before the purchase that Art heard about servant leadership for the first time from Ken Blanchard. Art had a heart for people, a head for numbers, and now, the tools necessary to transform an organization into servant leaders.

The miracle is that Art Barter ultimately bought Datron with no personal cash and with no venture capital, for about $15,000 in attorney fees.[6] How did it happen?

Art made an initial offer to Titan to purchase the company. Art didn't have the financial assets to make this purchase, so as Titan was mulling over the offer, he searched for investors nationally and internationally for the $1 million deposit Titan required.

During the negotiation period, a $7 million order came in for Datron products from the Republic of Zimbabwe. This land-locked African country, formerly called Southern Rhodesia, rarely had the financial capability to make such an investment for their police. To secure the order, the Republic of Zimbabwe offered a $2 million deposit to Datron, which they were willing to hold until after the sale was completed. Art, still an officer of Datron under Titan, did not believe that would be honest. He contacted the officials at Titan. Since the work would be performed by the newly purchased Datron, Titan agreed to receive $1 million of the $2 million from Zimbabwe as the down payment they were seeking. The final negotiated price between Titan and Transnortad was $4.7 million.[7] Art agreed. Within six months, Art Barter paid the full balance of the purchase price, and he was owner of Datron free of debt. Looking back on those events, Art and his wife, Lori, clearly believed the purchase was a miracle!

ADVERSITY COMES IN MANY FORMS

What can be learned about the art of servant leadership within the midst of adversity?

On March 20, 1980, after 123 years of silence, Mount St. Helens erupted in a 4.1 magnitude earthquake centered beneath the volcano. On March 30, a record seventy-nine earthquakes were recorded on the mountain. By April 3, the mountain had taken an eerie appearance because of ash-covered slopes. In late April, a significant bulge began to form, created by the building pressure of hot gases and magma inside the mountain. Finally, on May 18, 1981, at 8:32 a.m., a 5.1 magnitude quake struck one mile below the mountain. The north face of the mountain destabilized, causing the largest landslide in recorded history and removing 1,300 feet from the summit. The intense high pressure along with the high-temperature steam turned 70 percent of the snow and glacial ice on the mountain to water. At 175 miles per hour, a massive amount of rock, ash, water, and trees swept into Spirit Lake and down the north fork of the Toutle River Valley. Trees were uprooted and washed as far as 6 miles from the mountain; molten rock was hurled across the terrain at speeds up to 670 miles per hour due to the pyroclastic force.

Mount St. Helens provides a dramatic metaphor for the adversity that can strike within a corporation. Just ask the people of Datron:

The Earthquake

The company was accused of violating the Foreign Corrupt Practices Act by the U.S. government. International and national press portrayed Datron as guilty even before the investigation was completed. The executive team at Datron was divided with some running the company while others invested full-time hours complying with the investigators.

The Eruption

Communication silos were established across departments and blame orientation among the executives. Employees' job security was threatened because of investigation and dwindling sales. The Datron sales team struggled to reestablish relationships with international markets and the U.S. government.

The Erosion

A lack of trust existed within teams and within departments.

Leadership and employees lacked ownership concerning projects and products.

Employees lacked confidence in the senior management team.

How a corporation handles adversity, even as large as this metaphorical earthquake, is critical to its eventual success in overcoming disaster. Datron had not only to survive but to thrive under the adversity.

During difficult times, most companies will consider standard corrective options: cost reductions, cash and working capital management, organizational redesigns, and process improvements. Additionally, in an effort to reduce risk, the company might invest in customer retention strategies, managing credit, divesting programs, and securing additional lines of credit.[8] Eruptions and erosion are the natural consequences of significant earthquakes near volcanoes. The goal for any organization, even under severe stress, is to create and maintain a sustainable competitive advantage. However, like the aftermath of an earthquake, all the maps have changed. In the business world, the roads to the north have moved to the east, hills have become flatlands, and dry land is now under water. The only way to overcome these significant changes is to no longer trust the old maps, but to rely on the trusted compass. The compass will always point north regardless of changes in the traumatized terrain.

For Datron, that compass was servant leadership. In an interview with *BPM Magazine*, Art Barter discussed the compass:

> *My management team and I decided that we didn't want to operate our company in a short-term environment. We wanted to operate it in an environment where we were able to make decisions on what was best for the company, not only in the short term, but also on a long-term basis. We wanted to have a very high trust level with employees; we wanted our employees to know we cared about them and their families. During the first year, we put together a mission*

and purpose that was very short and to the point. Our purpose is to positively impact people's lives today and in the future, to leave the folks that we deal with better off than they were when they first met Datron. That's what we focused on.[9]

If the compass is servant leadership, then employees know which direction is true north. According to the compass, the executives and the employees place values in alignment with business behavioral strategies, entering new markets, enhancing customer offerings, exploring better margins through innovative models, partnering with suppliers and eliminating outdated sources. In spite of the climate changes within the business and the ever-changing global economy, the customer, the employee, and all the stakeholders can trust the integrity of the service provided. Servant leadership can provide the right kind of light to see farther into the future and with greater clarity than when the darkness of adversity strikes.

ADVERSITY REVEALS CHARACTER AND PROVIDES CREDIBILITY

Three significant aspects of adversity can be used as opportunities for the organization.

First, adversity paves the way for potential growth, internally and externally, individually and corporately. Many organizations, both for profit and nonprofit, place value on their employees based on only four criteria: "Do they make us money?," "Do they save us money?," "Do they increase our production?," or "Do they cut our costs?" There is nothing wrong with the questions, but they are not enough, because they are one-sided.

Some questions also to consider: "Are the employees growing professionally and personally?" "Are the employees learning new skill sets and developing values that produce civility and engage in greater life-promoting activities for family, friends, and colleagues?" "When the employees build a product, do they understand the big picture about why it can enhance the quality of life or save life?"

Asking only the first four questions suggests that leaders are more committed to transactional leadership than servant leadership. Transactional leadership supports the premise that employees are tools to utilize for corporate gain. Asking the second set of questions suggests a more transformational style of leadership that attempts to teach employees to be servant leaders. Adversity, under servant leaders, provides room for all to grow and learn from their experiences.

Just as we develop our physical muscles through overcoming opposition—such as lifting weights—we develop our character muscles by overcoming challenges and adversity.

Second, adversity provides the truth about us and others, in character, competency, and communication. Tough times can teach us much about ourselves as leaders. Sometimes the adversities seem to be unwarranted, meaningless, and beyond our control. These blows can knock our breath away individually and collectively. Other times, we are partly responsible for corporate calamity. Either way, the pain is real.

The one benefit of adversity is perspective. Adversity allows you the opportunity to see the truth about yourself and can provide you the opportunity to see the true characteristics of others. Adversity doesn't develop character as much as it reveals character. Adversity can point out areas for professional improvement or reveal unused skills. Adversity can teach us about the importance of relationships and the important keys toward effective communication with one another.

In times of adversity people spend more energy focusing on the facts of the current situation as opposed to what is true. Let me explain. My close friend Linnie Phelps helped me clarify the difference between truth, facts, and lies: Truth is able to stand alone; facts may be reality, but are always subject to interpretation; and lies always have a hidden agenda.

Under adversity, servant leaders first spend time in self-reflection, accepting appropriate responsibility and examining personal actions that may have contributed to the problem. They want the truth, so they spend no time distorting facts. They have no hidden agenda.

Art Barter said, "Part of helping employees succeed is building their trust in their managers and in the company. To do that, you have to be transparent. If people catch wind that what you're telling them isn't true, your credibility goes in the tank, and it's going to take you a long time to get that back. So I tell Datron's leaders to tell the employees the truth. You have to be courageous enough to have those tough discussions about truth."[10]

Finally, adversity produces clarity of purpose in our lives, helping us avoid diversions and provoking within us essential disciplines.

LIZ MURRAY AND METANOIA

A wonderful example of a new leader who turned adversity into opportunity is Liz Murray, a young woman with an engaging smile, energetic personality, and an awe-inspiring dream.[11] Liz grew up near Yankee Stadium with cocaine-addicted parents. Because her parents would choose the next high over the next meal, Liz and her sister were forced to eat from dumpsters. When Liz was sixteen years old, her mother died of AIDS, the result of too many dirty needles. Eventually, her father died of AIDS as well. Living on the streets, Liz would spend all day with her fellow homeless friends and all night on the subways to pass the time.

But *metanoia* happened to Liz Murray! Metanoia is an ancient Greek word that means a change of mind. Liz decided that she was not going to let the negative circumstances of her life control her. She didn't want to stay angry, or afraid, or emotionally paralyzed. She decided to make her life count! Liz Murray achieved clarity of purpose, ignoring all the diversions and focusing each day on one empowered choice after another.

Determined to take charge of her life, Liz begged several dozen high schools to let her back into the academic environment. Dozens turned her down, but she knew she only needed one school to accept her. Despite the lack of school transcripts and birth records, one school accepted her on probation. Liz finished her four-year high school program in two years, often sleeping on the streets near the campus.

During high school Liz visited Harvard on a school outing. She loved the ancient library and she loved the snow-covered architectural structures. She wanted to go to Harvard, but her pennies would not begin to cover the tuition. So she applied for an academic scholarship sponsored by *The New York Times* and won! Then she met with the admissions counselor at Harvard and got in! Now, Liz Murray is a graduate of one of the most distinguished universities in the United States.

What transformed her life from homeless to Harvard? As she says, "I realized that my life was my responsibility! It is my life. I can build my conversations around complaining and fill my thoughts with resentment, or I can choose to be grateful and work harder."

Liz Murray decided to live with clarity of purpose. Her empowered choices changed her life! The personal discipline needed to achieve her dream was a price she was willing to pay. Today Liz Murray is an inspirational leader helping thousands get back on their feet from adverse conditions.

Facing adversity is never easy and always comes with a degree of pain. Robert E. Lee knew adversity. Abraham Lincoln knew adversity. Liz Murray knew adversity. So did Art Barter and the Datron team. Overcoming the earthquakes, eruptions, and erosions caused by adversity can provide great opportunities to change your mind, develop previously unknown talents, and change your direction.

Table Talk

Discussing and Reflecting on Chapter 3

1. Your Personal Encounters with Adversity

In the last chapter, you noted your life's defining moments. Which of your defining moments were characterized by adversity? Are there other examples in your life in which you handled adversity but didn't think of them as defining moments? When you write about them, tell the story: what was happening, who was involved, what was required of you?

2. What You Learned, How You Grew

For each of these stories, identify what you discovered about yourself and what you learned. How was your *character* being tested: your integrity, your intent and motives? In what ways was your *competency* being tested: your talents, capabilities, and skills? What did you learn about yourself? How did these difficult experiences contribute to your personal growth and development? What strengths do you now have as a result of moving through these challenging experiences?

3. Your Organization's Encounters with Past Adversity

What kind of difficult challenges has your organization experienced in the past? Were these big events, earthquakes that suddenly exploded, or less obvious rumblings and shifts in the landscape that affected your organization? Were these events caused by external or internal focus?

4. Understanding Cause and Effect

What were the consequences of these adverse experiences? How did your organization's landscape change? Was the impact on the organization experienced as sudden eruptions of poor communication, misunderstandings, blame, finger-pointing, and conflict or more subtle erosions over time of people's loss of confidence and trust in each other and management?

5. Your Leadership Response

As a leader, how did you respond to these challenges? Looking back, were you part of the problem or a guide to the solution? What inner beliefs and values guided you? What external resources did you draw on that helped you? What did you learn? How did you grow and develop as a leader as a result of these experiences? Did your people also grow and develop in response to these challenges?

6. Your Present Stresses

What challenges does your organization face now? How has the landscape changed for your organization? What are the causes of these challenges? What impact are you seeing on people, processes, and products/services?

7. Communicating the Truth

In dealing with change and challenges, how effective have you been in communicating the truth about your own strengths and weaknesses and your understanding of your organization's strengths and weaknesses?

8. Your Leadership Compass

Based on your experience and what you have learned in dealing with adversity, what is your leadership compass? What guiding principles and values focus your leadership? How do your guiding principles and values reflect those of a servant leader?

9. Your Assessment

Servant leadership is an orientation to serving others and an intention to continually grow and develop as a leader, drawing on and learning from both the good and the difficult experiences in life. Place a check mark where you believe more reflection or action would be helpful in your journey.

❏ Noting down and reflecting on my personal experiences with adversity.

❏ Identifying how, specifically, these experiences helped build both my character and my competency.

❏ Recalling the history of my organization's experience of adversity and change.

❏ Understanding the impact of adversity and change on the people of my organization and their reactions, both negative and positive.

❏ Knowing when my own beliefs and behaviors have been part of the problem rather than a guide to solution.

❏ Being clear about my organization's present challenges and being willing to honestly communicate the truth about the nature and scope of these challenges.

❏ Having a clear leadership compass for guiding my organization that directly reflects my own guiding principles and values and my commitment to being of genuine service to others.

10. Your Summary

Based on this chapter's Table Talk, summarize the challenges your organization faces now. Describe your leadership compass in terms of how you will guide the changes that will be required in order to effectively respond to these challenges. Identify the specific character and skill-building competencies both you and the people of your organization need to develop or strengthen in this period.

4

Leading Yourself before Leading Others

Everyone thinks of changing the world,
but no one thinks of changing himself.
—Leo Tolstoy

Most of the corruption and disruption in corporations is the result of leaders' failure to lead themselves. Most leaders have a high drive for ambition and a low drive for mediocrity. They are usually fast paced and task oriented. Most of the time they have a need to be right, and in fact, concerning their company, they usually are right.

Like Alexander the Great in ancient times, they want to conquer their known world. And like Alexander, they often fail to conquer themselves. Alexander established an empire that stretched from Greece to India and spread the Greek culture throughout the known world at that time. Yet, he could not control himself and his excesses: his sexual appetite, explosive temper, increased paranoia, and mad drinking. His comprehensive power became quickly corrupted. His psychological state was characterized with delusions of grandeur as he sought to be worshipped as a living god. This Macedonian leader showed great potential as a youth, delivered great results as a military genius, and died in great mystery at the age of thirty-three.[1]

Art Barter is a man with a vision, a heart for people, and a head for numbers. But please don't get the impression, based on the first three chapters, that Art will soon be canonized for sainthood. He will tell you he is imperfect. Sometimes he is aware of his imperfections, and sometimes he doesn't realize the impact his imperfections have upon others on the Datron team. Servant leadership does not require perfection; what it needs is a process involving dignity and civility and competencies that will equip, inspire, and encourage others to become servant leaders. Art is dedicated to servant leadership but, at times, struggles to match his I.Q. with his I Do.

PROFILE OF AN IMPERFECT SERVANT LEADER

Art is a compassionate leader who is sensitive to the needs of others in the organization. During his best moments, Art listens to his colleagues and employees with genuine interest. Because of his concern for others, Art gives of himself and his dollars to those in need. Some say he is generous to a fault. Art is highly perceptive and intuitive to the mood within the organization. Art has been described as determined, persistent, and responsible. His finance background and track record within Datron have provided Art with a sense of confidence about his corporate decision-making abilities.

Art also worries. He worries about his company, his executives, his products, his customers, his family, and his health. Unfortunately, worry erodes self-esteem and personal confidence. Worry often leads people to question themselves or take more time to make significant decisions.

When Art became the new owner of Datron, he loved his newfound independence as owner and president. However, Art carried a heavy burden of responsibility for Datron's people and products.

Our personalities always provide us opportunities for personal growth and learning. Art is not an exception. The nurture associated with his finance and accounting education and experience only adds fuel to his analytical and critical nature. Art has said to others, "If you want me to make a decision about something that I don't have peace about, I am simply going to dig in my heels." Art wants to trust others, but, at times, struggles with trust. He will tell you it is because people have made promises they couldn't keep. That may be true, but it is also true that Art needs to be convinced more than most in moving in a different direction. The need to be convinced has worked in his favor with business and with people. At times, it has been a weakness. Like all of us, Art occasionally makes assumptions about people, misinterpreting their motives and challenging their ideas before they have been fully expressed.

THE COMPLEXITY OF LEADERSHIP PERSONALITIES

In philosophy and theology, scholars debate the status of human beings at birth: that is, are we born bad or good? However, both sides will ultimately agree that we are imperfect as human beings. Flawed, blemished, stained, and marred are other words that can describe our self-absorbed tendencies that lead to unhealthy thinking, unproductive relationships, and poor choices. When these behaviors increase in frequency and elevate in intensity, psychiatrists label them as psychological disorders.[2]

Most of us don't have psychological disorders, but we do have imperfect moments. It would be wonderful to have our imperfect moments occur only in private. However, our imperfections often seem to be brought out by those closest to us. Stressors at home and work often cause psychological buttons to be pushed within us. So, we act out inappropriately with our lips and inconsistently with our life values. As a result, we hurt our family, our friends, our colleagues, and ourselves. This paradox of personality is part of being human.

47

OUR HUMANITY IS FULLY REVEALED IN SERVANT LEADERSHIP

Followers forget that leaders are human. Followers can place unreasonable expectations and hold their leaders to impossible standards that they are unwilling to hold for themselves. They forget that everyone, including leaders, has two core needs in life: to love and be loved.

What does this have to do with leadership? Everything. What does this have to do with business? Again, everything. We are spiritual beings and social creatures. If you ignore our spirituality and our social needs, you will never be more than a transactional leader. Of course, people have other needs, for example, the need to create. But if you don't meet the indispensable need to love and be loved, the other needs will suffer, and we will be unable to live life fully.

The confusion for leaders is that the meaning of love has taken a beating. So much so that many in our society cannot tell the difference between the concepts of love, like, and lust. The ancient Greeks had several words for love, describing more clearly the difference between romance, friendship, and charity. The one word that best describes the heart of a servant leader is the Greek word *agape*. The word properly applied will describe the interrelationship between our psychological need to love and be loved, the rule of life in servant leadership, and the realities associated with the business world. *Agape* means to choose to seek the best for others. *Servant leadership is intentional action that seeks the best for others.*

Servant leadership is the only kind of leadership that recognizes the basic needs of all human beings. By its very nature, servant leadership is transformational, instead of transactional. Servant leadership is people driven, instead of project driven. Servant leadership allows everyone to win, instead of just the chosen few.

LEADING YOURSELF BENEFITS OTHERS

Lack of self-awareness can be painful. It can hurt you in the pocketbook and cost you the confidence of your personnel. The more unaware of themselves leaders are, the more they will use positional power instead of transformational power. They will find themselves using their position to coerce behavior and results, instead of equipping, inspiring, and encouraging those they influence to even greater heights. They are blind to their impact upon others.

Augustine of Hippo, one of the great minds in the early fifth century, wrote, "People travel to wonder at the height of mountains, at the huge waves of the sea, at the long courses of rivers, at the vast compass of the ocean, at the circular motion of the stars; and they pass by themselves without wondering."[3] Those very same words could be applied to us 1,600 years later!

All the great leaders and leadership experts acknowledge and teach the importance of self-awareness. John Maxwell says, "The first person we must examine is ourselves." He calls it the Mirror Principle.[4] Peter Senge calls it Personal Mastery.[5] Bill Hybels of *Courageous Leadership* calls it essential for full-leadership potential.[6] Steven Covey calls self-awareness the foundational component for developing emotional intelligence. In his famous book, *The Seven Habits of Highly Effective People,* the first chapter is all about self-awareness.[7] The Chairman and CEO of Starbucks, Howard Schultz, in his book *Pour Your Heart Into It*, describes how self-awareness propelled him forward to the success he is having today.[8] Even the Babe Ruth of corporate management, Jack Welch, speaks of self-awareness in his book, *Jack: Straight from the Gut.*[9]

THE SEVEN ESSENTIAL ELEMENTS OF LEADING YOURSELF

So how do you lead yourself? It requires a willingness to practice these seven essential elements.

The Art of Servant Leadership

Ask Yourself Questions

- Benjamin Franklin was one of the great leaders at one of the most critical times in the United States. Brilliant in science and politics, Franklin believed the source of his success was directly attributed to the power of the question in self-reflection. So he listed thirteen virtues that he wanted to acquire (moderation, cleanliness, sincerity, and so on). Each day he devoted his reflection to one of these virtues. He considered his behavior regarding that virtue for the day and recorded any faults he found in a little book. Here are some of his essential virtues along with the questions he would ask himself in his personal reflection:[10]

- Resolution: Did I perform what I ought; did I perform without fail what I resolved?

- Frugality: Did I do good to others; did I waste nothing?

- Industry: Did I lose no time; was I always employed in something useful and cut off all unnecessary actions?

- Justice: Did I wrong none by doing injuries, or omitting the benefits that are my duty?

In the same way, you can ask yourself questions like these as a servant leader:

- What gifts have I received from others today? (for example, gifts of time, talent, tongue, or treasure)

- What gifts have I given to others today?

- What did I say or do that caused unnecessary pain for others?

- How did I serve others? In joy and peace or anger and worry?

Leading yourself starts with your willingness to ask questions about how you think, feel, do, and say.

Be Silent

Most people are not really interested in honest feedback. Many times they are asking for feedback in order to receive an affirmation. When they are surprised at the feedback, they tend to rationalize the responses, justify their actions, and even get angry at the comments. People around them learn not to provide accurate feedback.

If you receive feedback with grace and dignity, on the other hand, others will be honest with you. So start with silence and listen to understand so that others will be encouraged to share with you. The silence must continue inside your head as well. Suspend judgment and listen. The silence must not only come from your lips and inner voice but also from your body language. You share meaning in your body language. If your voice is silent, but your facial gestures or hand movements indicate disapproval, you are not going to get honest feedback in the future. After silence, then summarize the feedback, show appreciation for it and reflect later on the accuracy of the comments. Remember, feedback isn't necessarily correct information. You can determine the accuracy of the comments by asking others who will be honest with you. But if you want feedback, silence is essential.

Be Vulnerable

Behind every sin is a wound that needs to be healed. Sin is what turns us away from living as we have been designed to live. Sin has many names. The clinical world may use the word addictions. The biblical world would use the word idolatry. The philosophical world would use the word attachments. The business world would use the word control. Our addictions, idols, attachments, and controlling behaviors are what turn us away from experiencing our basic needs in life: to love and be loved.

The wounds, if untreated, create for all human beings self-deception and increasing tolerance for unhealthy behavior. They cause an absence of focus and a loss of willpower. Because of the power of our personal wounds behind our sins, we become experts in rationalizing, repressing, justifying, and excusing our behaviors that hinder us from experiencing transforming leadership and liberating followership.

Now, please don't misunderstand. You don't need to reveal your darkest secrets or deepest wounds to everyone in the office. I am not promoting corporate psychotherapy sessions. However, leadership, in particular, servant leadership, cannot be accomplished successfully until you learn to lead yourself. Others in your organization will not respect your leadership until you are willing to inspect yourself. Vulnerability is the willingness to be out in the open as a human leader. That vulnerability brings transparency, genuineness, and authenticity to the life principles you hold dear. Only through the journey of self-discovery can you maximize your strengths and minimize your weaknesses as a leader. You can only lead others as far as you are willing to go.

Hear from the Community

Most leaders struggle with community. They think communities move too slowly, think too superficially, and speak too casually about important priorities. Communities tend to resist change and like the status quo. Leaders become impatient with the lack of urgency within communities. However, what communities bring to leaders is accountability, and what they teach leaders is patience.

Power in the hands of any imperfect human being ultimately will be self-destructive without accountability. The American government, for example, is full of checks and balances because too much power unchecked is a guarantee for disaster.

Leaders have the uncanny ability to receive revelations that provide special insights concerning a problem or a special vision to go forward. However, the trusted community can provide you with the right interpretation of that revelation. Communities create an environment where the leader can think through the implications of their decisions and their impending actions. Basically, a community is a group of people who have a shared interest in your success. They may be your professional colleagues or simply personal friends that have an understanding of your background. Occasionally, they may even be astute family members.

Here are some tips about choosing your community:

- Choose those in your community who are with you the most, not those who see you the least.

- Choose those in your community who can see you at your worst, not just those who see you at your best.

- Choose those in your community who you are willing to eat with or play with, not just those you are willing to work with.

- Choose those in your community whom you respect for their integrity, not just those you admire for their accomplishments.

- Choose those in your community who are willing to listen to understand, not just those who want to be understood.

- Choose those in your community who care about you as a person, not just those who care about you professionally.

- Choose those in your community who are willing to ask the tough questions, not just those who provide the easy answers.

- Choose those in your community who maintain confidentiality, not just those who are compelling in personality.

Love Preparation

On January 15, 2009, U.S. Airways Flight 1549, heading to Charlotte, North Carolina, from New York's LaGuardia Airport had to make an emergency landing into a chilly Hudson River because a flock of birds struck both engines after takeoff. The plane was airborne less than three minutes. The pilot, fifty-seven-year-old Chesley "Sully" Sullenberger, steered the crippled Airbus A320 to a textbook emergency landing. This "miracle on the Hudson" was the result of preparation. Sullenberger knew his aircraft, his copilot, and himself, knowledge that paid immense dividends in the midst of the crisis. His preparation saved the lives of 155 people.

However, it wasn't his experience in water landings that did it! Former Delta pilot Denny Walsh said, "You really don't practice water landings in commercial airplanes. Just the sheer expertise he demonstrated is amazing."

How did the expertise happen? Preparation. Just check the facts:[11]

- Sully served as a fighter pilot for nearly seven years in the U.S. Air Force

- He served as Air Line Pilots Association safety chairman, accident investigator, and national technical committee member.

- He developed new protocols for airline safety for the U.S. Air Force and the National Transportation Safety Board.

- He was visiting scholar at the University of California, Berkeley, at the Center for Catastrophic Risk Management.

- He earned two master's degrees (industrial psychology and public administration) and a bachelor's degree from the Air Force Academy in Colorado Springs, Colorado.

- He has been a U.S. Airways pilot since 1980.

Chesley B. Sullenberger III was prepared to handle a disaster. He had never landed an eighty-one-ton plane in the Hudson River in the past and he hopes he never will in the future. His preparation through the years provided him with the necessary knowledge to know himself, his team, and his plane.

Preparation means that you are always growing and learning. Education just doesn't stop when you leave the classroom in your twenties. It also continues when you read the works of great thinkers on leadership, biographies about great leaders, and critically assess your own strengths and weaknesses through training events, forums, and psychological tools that enhance performance. Learning also comes from teaching. I often tell my students that I learn more through preparing and teaching in graduate school than when I attended graduate school myself.

Develop New Habits

Our thinking about life will eventually show in our actions in life. Our individual actions in life will accumulate to create a pattern of living. Our pattern of living will provide a long-lasting imprint of character. And that imprint of character will often determine our future fate. I am not alone in this conviction.

According to Ralph Waldo Emerson, "Sow a thought and you reap an action; sow an act and you reap a habit; sow a habit and you reap a character; sow a character and you reap a destiny."[12] "Motivation is what gets you started. Habit is what keeps you going," Jim Ryun, Olympic athlete said.[13] And Stephen R. Covey wrote, "Our character is basically a composite of our habits. Because they are consistent, often unconscious patterns, they constantly, daily, express our character."[14]

Character forms whether we intend it to or not. We are influenced constantly from our environment, and our tendency is to choose the road of passively receiving the stimulus. However, this affects how we think, how we feel, and what we do. The right kind of character formation has to be intentional and habitual. The ability to know ourselves and lead ourselves can only happen if we develop a lifestyle of self-discipline. We need to be intentional about developing healthy habits: physically, emotionally, relationally, psychologically, and professionally.

Habits are habit forming. So start small to ensure success. Write down the counter-productive habits in your life. State clearly in one sentence what new habit you would like to create to eradicate the old negative habit. Stay diligent with this new habit for thirty days. Share with your professional community, and especially your chosen trusted partners in your journey as a leader, your desire and your game plan.

You will find that if you work on one habit some other counterproductive habits will naturally change as well. For example, if you develop a new habit of daily exercise for your physical well-being, the exercise also will benefit your attitude and increase your energy level. Or if you work to learn how leaders lead effectively, the information you absorb naturally will help you to develop qualities in building relationships and influencing people. The key is that you must be intentional!

Commit for the Long Term

Servant leaders are committed to people and process. They are not looking for short-term gains at the expense of long-term benefits. People need time to trust. The CEO needs time to understand.

All effective leaders know their people. They care. The temptation for the executives at a public company is to be a slave to the stock market and the financial analyst. Leadership is about relationships, not NASDAQ.

If leadership is simply the art of influence, or applied power, one can rely on positional power to coerce followers or manipulate other leaders to do what you want. The keys for positional power are well known. Positional power is determined by how central your role is within the organization, how visible you are with the senior executives, and how relevant your skills and expertise are with the current organizational priorities. But servant leadership is applied power with a moral imperative. And that moral imperative within leadership is to serve for the sake of others. Fulfilling that vision moves leaders from transactional relationships with their coworkers to transformational relationships that will improve them and you.

Like us, Art Barter is a paradox of personality. But he is growing and learning because he understands the need for self-awareness. If you want to be a servant leader, it will mean that all your life you must be growing and learning. Ten years from now, Art will be closer to the servant leader he wants to be. But he will still be growing and learning.

Hundreds of books speak of the critical need for self-awareness. This is because the biggest obstacle of leadership truly is us, ourselves. Once we know that truth, and are willing to grow and learn, we are 90 percent on the way to being a successful servant leader!

Table Talk

Discussing and Reflecting on Chapter 4

1. Your Self-Awareness as a Leader

Think about your imperfections and flaws as a leader. How aware are you of your weaknesses? What are your weaknesses?

2. Your Worries

What things do you worry about? What are the repeating themes of your worries?

3. Your Imperfect Moments

What people or situations trigger you and cause you to react emotionally in a way that can have negative impact? What, specifically, is the impact on others? On yourself? For example, do you lose patience and blame others when your expectations are not met? Do you regret these outbursts? Do they get you the outcomes you really want? Describe the type of people and situations that are emotional triggers for you.

4. Your Insights

What insights do you have regarding your worries and your imperfect moments? What connections can you make between the two? For example, you may worry that as a leader you don't know enough, and you doubt your capability at times. If someone questions you about an area in which you feel inadequate, you may react defensively.

5. Your Accountability

How aware are you of internal thought processes and emotional responses? What inner self-talk do you use when your mind is full of worried thoughts? Can you quiet your mind? Are you aware of what is happening inside of you when another person or situation triggers you emotionally? Does your ego feel threatened? What do you do to gain control of your emotions and seek mutual benefit, win-win outcomes?

6. Self-Reflection Questions

How do your values represent key virtues? Think of these virtues: faith, hope, love, wisdom, justice, courage, moderation. If you were to ask yourself at the end of each day if you were able to lead from your values and demonstrate them in your actions, what virtues would be evident? For example, if your value is to help and serve others, the virtue you want to demonstrate in everyday choices and actions is seeking the best for others, or love. Revisit Ben Franklin's personal reflection questions and then write at least three self-reflection questions you could ask yourself at the end of each day, starting with "Did I…?"

7. Use of Silence

How do you use silence in your life? What parts of your day include silence and reflection? Do you need to put more moments of silence in your life? What times of day would be best for you? Think of using your self-reflection questions in these periods of quiet.

8. Seeking Feedback, Being Vulnerable

How often do you ask for feedback on your leadership effectiveness and from whom? Are you able to be silent and genuinely listen to what is being said without being defensive? Are you willing to seriously consider other viewpoints and ideas? Are you able to openly admit mistakes? Do you see being vulnerable as a weakness or as a strength? How could you improve in this area, and how would those improvements transform you as a leader?

9. Knowing Your Community

How would you describe your community? Who is in it? Think of trusted relationships at work and in your life. On whom do you depend to ask the tough questions and give you honest feedback? Whose input, ideas, and suggestions have expanded your way of seeing and being in the world as a leader? How could you expand and deepen the use of these resources? What people would be particularly helpful to you now?

10. Continual Preparation

What are your sources of inspiration and continual learning in this period of your life? Who are your role models and teachers? If you could choose any resource that would expand your leadership competence in this period, what resources, vehicles, or tools would you use?

11. Helpful Habits

What are your counterproductive habits? In what ways are they connected to your leadership weaknesses? If you were to replace these habits with new, productive habits, what would they be? Spend a few moments describing the new habits and how they would benefit you and enrich your life.

12. Your Assessment

Servant Leaders have self-awareness. They are willing to be vulnerable; they hold themselves accountable to their values and recognize the power of continual transformation through self-reflection, continual learning, and renewal. Place a check mark where you believe more reflection or action would be helpful in your journey:

❏ Improving my awareness of my weaknesses as a leader.

❑ Seeing the connection between my worries and my imperfect moments.

❑ Being more accountable for my ego-driven, emotional responses.

❑ Using self-reflection questions based on my values every day.

❑ Being willing to use silence and actively seek feedback.

❑ Knowing and using trusted people in my community to expand my growth and development as a leader.

❑ Making and keeping commitments to continual learning and continual preparation.

❑ Replacing counterproductive habits with life-enhancing habits.

13. Your Summary

Based on this chapter's Table Talk, summarize your intentions to continue to grow and develop as a servant leader.

Part 2

THE FORMULA FOR SUCCESS: LIVING FOR THE SAKE OF OTHERS

5

Creating a Servant Leadership Culture

In the transmission of human culture, people always attempt to replicate,
to pass on to the next generation the skills and values of the parents, but the
attempt always fails because cultural transmission
is geared to learning, not DNA.

—GREGORY BATESON

In the sterile and unfamiliar environment of a hospital room, it is often difficult for grieving families to express their love openly to those who are dying. Fortunately for Carmen Lesso, she was able to hold her husband's hand and watch him take his last breath at home—in his own bed. Surrounded by family members, including her two adult children, Carmen whispered her last words to her beloved husband, Juan.

Fifteen miles southeast of her home, her fellow Datron employees were busy at work. Some were chatting in the break room about the recent front-page news that San Diego Gas & Electric was raising their rates again while others were busy on the assembly room floor putting together the military radios. Nearly all the employees on that Tuesday morning were thinking about Carmen, who was known for her thirty years of faithful service and viewed lovingly as the "queen mother" within Datron.

Carmen's paid time off (PTO) benefit had long since been used. But the employees and the executives at Datron happily contributed their personal PTO to Carmen so she could spend time with her husband. Such gestures have been repeated by many employees from other companies in the past. But caring deeds like these are at the very core of Datron World Communications.

Many factors contribute to creating a flourishing, vital organization. Effective corporations weigh their success equally between people and performance. They disagree with Milton Friedman's famous remark that "a corporation's sole public responsibility is the maximization of profits."[1] At Datron, the dignity of the human being is as important for the welfare of the organization as the efficiency of the company.

WHAT IS CORPORATE CULTURE?

The origin of the word culture comes from the Latin *cultura*. It means "cultivation of the soil." We still use it in the original sense when we speak of agriculture. The word was used for the first time in 1510 metaphorically to describe "cultivation through education." Cultivating the mind suggested the development and improvement of the intellectual side of the person. Ray Bradbury, the American science fiction novelist, used the word culture in that sense when he wrote, "You don't have to burn books to destroy a culture. Just get people to stop reading them."[2] By the mid eighteenth century, culture was more globally defined as the collective customs and achievements of a group of people, more or less identical with the concept of civilization.

You can see how the concept of culture can be difficult to define. Biologists used the word to describe the growth of living cells and tissues under strict laboratory conditions. Anthropologists, sociologists, psychologists, political scientists, economists, organizational specialists, and social scientists all use the word without providing a clear and concise definition to the public.

Culture is a term that connotes different things to different people. Because there is lack of clarity, the term corporate culture can confuse the chief executive officer and the human resource director as much as the hourly worker on the assembly floor

Here is my definition.

Corporate culture is a way of life cultivated over time through shared experiences, values, and behaviors.

This definition probably raises questions in your mind. How do I develop the right kind of corporate culture? What way of life do I want to create? Regardless of corporate position, what do we all embrace, experience, or express? Whatever the corporate culture is in your organization, it will definitely shape your vision, values, goals, attitudes, behavior, and voice. Corporate culture is often shaped and sustained by workplace rituals, ceremonies, and group affirmations. Corporate culture can even affect the bottom line of an organization. For example, in my opinion, corporate culture was the primary factor in the scandals at Enron Corporation and WorldCom.

CORPORATE CULTURE IS A WAY OF LIFE

How do you cultivate a new way of life for a corporation? The new corporate way of life has to be nurtured and developed over time. The cultivation is the process by which a corporation, along with its people, becomes all that they are capable of being.

The concept comes from farming, where cultivation is a five-stage process:

1. Clean the environment. Remove the unnecessary debris from the soil, including weeds and rocks that will hinder growth of the seed.

2. Till the ground. Break up the soil so that the ground can be receptive to receiving the seeds. This may include adding some new topsoil to aid the process of growth.

3. Sow the seeds. This requires knowledge about the needs of different kinds of seeds. Corn, squash, tomatoes, and carrots all grow best when seeds are planted the right distance from each other, and in the right depth and location.

4. Tend the garden. Nurture the garden with the right amount of water and nutrients, and make sure the garden gets the proper amount of sunlight.

5. Guard the garden. Protect the garden from insects and other intruders that simply seek to destroy your garden for their own self-interests.

Clean, till, sow, tend, and guard are good active verbs describing the stages of cultivation for a farmer or for a corporate executive. Most organizations don't consciously try to create a certain culture. As a result, the organization's culture is defined by money. Greed defines its values. Results are all that matters. That kind of thinking is self-destructive for the organization and for the individual.

Southwest Airlines takes a different approach. The organization invests in developing a culture. They are intentional about how they do business, how they relate to one another, and how they relate to their customers. Doing the right thing is more than a slogan at Southwest, it is their way of life. For the thirteenth year in a row, *Fortune* magazine recognized Southwest for their outstanding achievements. They are the only airline to make the top ten list of the world's most admired companies.[3] Herb Kelleher, cofounder and chairman emeritus of Southwest Airlines, describes how they were able to maintain their culture. In his comments you can pick out the five stages of cultivation:

First of all, it starts with hiring. We are zealous about hiring. We are looking for a particular type of person, regardless of which job category it is. We are looking for attitudes that are positive and for people who can lend themselves to causes ... If you start with the type of person you want to hire, presumably you can build a work force that is prepared for the culture you desire.

Another important thing is to spend a lot of time with your people and to communicate with them in a variety of ways. And a large part of it is demeanor ... we want our management to radiate the demeanor that we are proud of our people, we are interested in them as individuals, and we are interested in them outside the work force, including the good and bad things that happen to them as individuals.[4]

Southwest Airlines knows how to cultivate a way of life. They describe their way of life as a fulfillment of the Golden Rule, which means treating others the way you want to be treated. Southwest lives that out by having a warrior spirit, servant's heart, and a fun-LUVing attitude.[5]

Like Southwest Airlines, Datron is committed to carefully cultivating its way of life. Datron believes that servant leadership is the only model for cultivating a culture that improves and enhances people and products, character and company, and communities and charities. However, this was not always the case. Jim Dowling describes the culture of Datron before servant leadership became the intentional goal. "I used to view work as an unpleasant chore and didn't particularly enjoy my job. I saw no interest in creating relationships with anyone as it was just a waste of time. It would only keep me from completing my tasks. I was all about driving for results and had been promoted in the past for that kind of behavior. I would hide my mistakes and grab as much recognition as I could to justify my position."[6]

Jim was not alone. His conduct was consistent with the overall culture of Datron. The philosophy and practices of the company told the employees that monetary results mattered more than people. As a result, inappropriate language was common in the workplace, drug use was rampant, and unprofessional behavior was tolerated. Then servant leadership was introduced by Art Barter. At first, Jim was not a believer in servant leadership. "When Art introduced servant leadership into Datron, I thought, 'Great! A new flavor-of-the-month concept.' I planned on giving it the same appearance of compliance I had always done on similar top management-led initiatives. Quickly this became different as we were expected to be graded by our peers on servant leadership behavior and were expected to create an action plan to improve."[7]

Jim understood that upper management had the power to enforce compliance but not cooperation. Jim was also aware that although management often encouraged new training programs, they would not be personally invested in the training.

Most new training comes because of the latest book from workplace consultants. A book that intrigued someone in the corporate office is introduced as a company guide in hopes that this will be the silver bullet to end all corporate suffering. No one on the assembly line is fooled. They believe that the training offered is simply another manipulative method to maximize profits. They think, "Management is not personally invested in changing, so why should we?" But this time Datron took a different approach. Datron seemed to be invested for the long-term and committed to the idea that everyone would practice servant leadership, including the highest levels of management.

Jim writes, "I thought I'd better take this seriously and found some material to help me. I came across John Maxwell's *21 Irrefutable Laws of Leadership* … As I read, I began to understand what people expected

70

in a leader and why they followed a leader. Although my negative behavior was somehow getting results, the results were at a cost and not sustainable. I was using people as tools and I relied solely on my title to influence others."

Jim continued to read about servant leadership and practice new skills. "As I began practicing these behaviors and holding myself accountable for bad behavior, I noticed how differently my staff began responding to me. Over time I also noticed improved performance on their part and also with myself … My staff seemed happier and so was I. This, of course, encouraged me to keep learning and practicing."[8]

CORPORATION AS COMMUNITY

Every corporation is a community that has shared beliefs, shared experiences, and shared expressions. They can be negative values and destructive practices, or they can be positive values and healthy practices. Regardless, the culture, whether healthy or unhealthy, is reinforced by those sharing their beliefs, experiences, and expressions. Every corporation must share the following as a minimum for sustaining a healthy environment.

Shared Beliefs

Rarely does anyone change because of information sent to the head. But if you can reach down fifteen inches to the heart of a person, then it becomes a mandate, a mission, and a cause that builds momentum. For cultural vitality, members of the corporate community must embrace

- The equality and worthiness of every human being

- The core need for everyone to be loved and to love

- The dignity of work for the benefit of self and others

71

Shared Experiences

Shared experiences touch the will of each individual and incorporate each individual mind to think as part of a unified group. For cultural vitality, members of the corporate community must experience

- Success as a team

- Failure as a team

- Being served by others

- Serving others

- Creative moments and productive time

- Rituals, rewards, and ceremonies consistently

- Balance between home and work

Shared Expressions

Shared expressions become the voice of the community and a verbal commitment to do what they know they can do. Members of the corporate community must express

- Joyful celebrations of accomplishments as a team

- Honest conversations without anger or resentment

- Appreciation and gratitude for the corporate family

- A desire for continual improvement in what they do and who they are

THE CULTURAL ARCHITECT

The main purpose of an architect is to produce a design for a physical structure with the aesthetic, structural, and safety features that must go into a construction of a building. Architects give that building a form. Most great architects are part psychologist and part artist. They are part psychologist because they spend a great deal of time analyzing human behavior, determining what the clients really want, and providing them choices concerning possible options. That they are also part artist is clear to anyone who sees a majestic skyline or a beautiful atrium. Architects are also very practical. They manage to place the fire exits, restrooms, and elevators close enough to all the offices and in full compliance with the current Americans with Disabilities Act standards.

Cultural architects are similar to structural architects in that they too are part psychologist and part artist. The cultural architect as psychologist must understand human behavior, systems theory, group dynamics, communication techniques, and conflict resolution. The artist within them focuses on the people and the corporation in developing the desired result. What matters to a corporate architect who is totally committed to servant leadership?

DESIGN MATTERS

Design matters in servant leadership. Steve Jobs, Apple founder and guru, says that "design is the fundamental soul of a man-made creation that ends up expressing itself in successive outer layers of the product or service."[9] Design reveals the organization's true trademark. For Datron, the true trademark is servant leadership.

The single most important concept in design is unity. A single message needs to be created within the facility itself and among the people themselves. The cultural architect must have a clear starting point, making sure that the individual elements of the program will not dominate the overall design of the organization. The corporation needs a clear, simple, and unified message.

The facilities need to be in alignment with the internal purpose of the company. The paintings and the furnishings must fit the message. While there is nothing wrong with variety, the executives and employees must have a sense that one message lies within the variety of the designs. What we care about must be on our shelves and on our walls. It must be in the office where the suits are and on the assembly floor where smocks are worn. People need to see and feel an atmosphere that suggests care, communication, and commitment to servant leadership for the benefit of others.

As you enter the modest lobby of Datron, you will encounter the motto of Datron, "In God we trust, In people we invest" posted on the wall. That trust and investment is seen on the walls in letters from nonprofit organizations around the world expressing their gratitude to Art Barter and the Datron employees for their financial assistance.

But the design is more than cosmetic fixtures and letters of appreciation. The design also includes people. The design is evident in a monthly celebration as Art Barter hands a bonus check of $13,000 (the equivalent of one-third of the employee's yearly salary) to an employee for coming up with an idea to save Datron some unnecessary expenses. It is evident in the yearly paid Hawaii trip for the leadership council and their spouses, composed of executives and nonexecutives, with a featured speaker on leadership. It is also seen in the unusually large training budget for servant leadership, which also includes life development and financial management skills.

PEOPLE MATTER

Great servant leaders develop their followers into servant leaders themselves. The cultural architect looks for those within the organization who are already demonstrating servant leadership behaviors. They know that servant leaders inspire others to follow and model their principles and practices. Servant leaders are never threatened by others with great potential. In fact, they are drawn to them and willing to give their power away to enhance their growth. Dr. Peter Drucker, the foremost academic guru on leadership in the twentieth century, once said, "There is no success without a successor."[10] The servant leader produces successors!

Someone asked me, what kind of people do I look for when I recruit? I said, smiling, "F.A.T. people." The person wasn't insulted. In fact, he knew I struggled with my waistline far more often than he did. So he said, "Seriously, how do you choose?"

I told him that the idea wasn't original with me. In fact, I learned it in my teens from my pastor, who said, "When I look for people, I look for those faithful, available, and teachable."

So when I recruit, I look for people who are

- Faithful to the principles of a more experienced servant leader

- Available to model the practices of a more experienced servant leader

- Teachable and ready to learn the proclamations of a more experienced servant leader

The most difficult pond in which to capture servant leaders is not at the highest levels of corporate America or even at the lowest. It is usually at the level of frontline supervisors or middle level managers where I have the most trouble in recruiting servant leaders. I am not alone.

The greatest areas of conflict, the greatest problems for communication, and the greatest need for personal control are usually lower middle management and frontline supervisory positions. They have a difficult time buying servant leadership or, for that matter, any other type of leadership that is not their own. They have seen the underbelly of upper management. They have worked their way up to have some sense of control and power. And information for them is power.

Often, they are not given the same amount of training in conflict resolution and communication styles as upper level management. They lack a global perspective on how their department impacts the overall health of the company. Many times they are not told why they should change their priorities on the floor or receive feedback on their suggestions.

I am not blaming them. I am simply identifying the problem. For years, they have seen themselves as just tools within the organization. But for a company committed to a new way, they will be the backbone that sustains and gives support to the framework of authentic servant leadership.

I fish for these servant leaders in two ways. First, I mentor servant leaders who fish daily in that pond. I teach them to look for faithful, available, and teachable people. Second, I look for aspiring servant leaders during our training sessions. Our team of trainers notices those who have really responded to concepts of servant leadership. Then we engage, invest, expose, and influence these people.

MOMENTUM MATTERS

In the last ten years, two books hit the national bestseller list that show how small things can make a big impact. *The Tipping Point*, by Malcolm Gladwell, describes how certain corporate ideas, products, messages, and behaviors became economic epidemics in society. Virtually overnight, they became household names. The three characteristics of viral epidemics are the same in business epidemics: they are contagious; little changes have big effects; and change happens dramatically, not gradually.[11] The tipping point is the greatest catalyst for change. Water boils at 212 degrees, not 211 degrees. Touchdowns are made in the end zone, not the one yard line. Momentum shifts when the team scores, not when they almost score.

Linda Kaplan Thaler and Robin Koval are authors of an instant best seller that affirms the principles of Malcolm Gladwell. The book is entitled *The Power of Small: Why Little Things Make All the Difference.* They believe, and rightly so, that seemingly small, insignificant actions can provide tremendous vehicles for growth and change.[12] The formula has been taught in high school physics classes around the world: Momentum equals mass times velocity (p = mv).

Enlarge the mass by enlisting the right people and more people. Increase the velocity by teaching servant leadership through many venues so that people can hear it, touch it, feel it, smell it, and taste it. Momentum becomes your greatest friend as a change agent.

EDUCATION MATTERS

Leaders must believe in education. If the key of real estate is location, location, location, the key for developing a servant leadership culture is training, training, training.

According to servant leadership thought leaders Ann McGee-Cooper and Gary Looper, TD Industries understands the importance of training. TD Industries is a mechanical and electrical construction and service company headquartered in Dallas, Texas, that is deeply committed to developing a servant leadership culture. They have a five-part strategy in their training:[13]

- Build a curriculum of servant-leadership work. TD has created day-long learning experiences to introduce and grow servant-leaders in the company. Materials, videos, and simulation games are some of the tools used in the learning experience.

- Build a foundation of credibility in the process. Senior leaders within TD introduce every class to call attention to the commitment within the company to servant leadership. Mid-level influential leaders co-teach the classes with the outside instructors and openly discuss their own corporate journeys. They link their personal experiences of servant leadership with genuine business challenges.

- Integrate servant leadership into other skill-based training programs. Every organization provides mandated training legislated by federal or state laws and has specialized elective training in skill development for their employees. TD integrates servant leadership into all of their training programs.

- Solicit feedback in order to fine-tune the learning experience. In an effort to provide continuous improvement, the participants provide feedback to the instructors and facilitators on ways to improve the learning experience.

- Implement a personal accountability program. Participants choose the new behavior or skill they would like to develop over the next three months. The learning process takes on three phases: initial training, ninety days of practice, and a final gathering to share accomplishments.

In the same way, Datron World Communications is committed to learning. Here is how Datron has committed to the learning process.

Datron developed a three-tiered curriculum for servant leadership. Each level is fifteen hours of training over a five-week period (three hours a week). The first level introduces the concept of servant leadership and helps participants see through the servant leader's lens. This section also covers the value system of Datron and the essential key for servant leadership, trust.

The second section is designed to develop your sense of value to yourself, others, and Datron by recognizing the strengths you already have as a servant leader. This section also discusses the impact of culture and the ability of one person to change the system. It covers the seven servant leadership virtues necessary to transform belief and behaviors.

Level 1 is designed to help the atheist, agnostic, or seeker of servant leadership to understand the significance servant leaders can make in their own life and the lives of others. Level 2 is designed to transform the seeker into a life-long learner of servant leadership. This is the discipleship phase of the learning experience.

Finally, at Level 3, the goal is to create apostles. Apostles simply mean sent-out ones. So Level 3 is designed to enhance participants' capability as servant leaders, overcome their personal roadblocks, and show them how to create a servant leadership culture in their professional and personal environment for the sake of others. This three-part training program is a requirement for all employees, regardless of position, at Datron.

Datron servant leaders are incorporated into the training: Like TD, Datron is committed to reinforcing the principles of servant leadership through the lives of people who are committed to being servant leaders. Videos of comments by servant leaders within Datron, presentations and introductions by senior staff, and co-teaching opportunities are presented.

Datron established the Servant Leadership Institute for organizations around the world. The mission and purpose of the Servant Leadership Institute is to create servant leaders that will transform organizations.[14] Publications and training manuals are available, along with an interactive website designed to make better servant leaders.[15] The institute was designed as Datron's gift to corporations, nonprofits, academic institutions, and communities in an effort to make this world a better place to live and work.

The Art of Servant Leadership

The Servant Leadership Training Institute has become a college of learning for all the employees in all facets of work and life skill development. Even on subjects as wide as diversity, quality control, or lean manufacturing, servant leadership is the core theme on why the organization does what it does. The training budget of Datron is significant, but the dividends pay off tenfold. In addition, small accountability groups within Datron focus on behavioral improvements and increasing shared experiences through corporate challenges.

Finally, Datron solicits feedback through various communication channels. For example, feedback may come in the biyearly surveys designed to measure the level of trust in the organization, or through group lunches with the president to discuss servant leadership. Feedback is encouraged and documented by trainers and facilitators at all three levels of training, and servant leadership is discussed at every senior executive gathering.

Datron understands that leadership is a learned behavior. Everyone is acknowledged as a leader because everyone has influence over others. So, it is not really if you are a leader, but how you lead that becomes the critical issue.

CARMEN LESSO, JIM DOWLING, AND SERVANT LEADERSHIP

Carmen Lesso, who lost her husband to pancreatic cancer, doesn't understand every technical aspect of servant leadership, but she knows when it is present. She knew servant leadership was not present at her company when the employees were treated as human tools to achieve financial results. Carmen thought all companies behaved in this way, so leaving was not the answer, and complaining would be the quickest way to lose her job.

She is learning how to be a servant leader. Now she knows that people and corporations can be different. She also knows that people want to work, live, and thrive in a servant leadership culture. She saw signs of it when Datron spontaneously reached out to her during the loss of her husband. She knew that her Datron family cared!

Jim Dowling, the manufacturing engineer, is an example of someone who has changed from being self-absorbed to working as a servant leader for the benefit of others. At first, Jim gave lip service to the concept of servant leadership so that his superiors would not bother him. Now Jim's path has taken him from an agnostic to a seeker, and he is moving from a disciple to an apostle of servant leadership.

The key was the cultural architect. In Datron's case, that cultural architect was Art Barter. Of course, he had help from skillful consultants and trainers, but as the CEO, it was essential that servant leadership was more than just a concept to him. It had to be reflected in design, in people, in commitment to its principles, and reinforced through education.

Table Talk

Discussing and Reflecting on Chapter 5

1. Cultural Architect: Whose Role Is It?

Do you see yourself as the cultural architect of your organization? Are you intentionally seeking to create an organizational culture, a way of life that all people understand and can embrace, based on clear values, shared experiences, and supportive behaviors? What strengths do you bring to this role? What constraints or concerns do you have?

2. Your Unifying Message

What is the most important, unifying message you can send your people that embodies the way of life you want all people in the organization to embrace, experience, and express? How would you describe your personal philosophy that lies behind this message?

3. Your Organization's Strengths

Have you and your leadership team identified your organization's strengths? What are they?

4. Your Mission

What is the stated purpose or mission of your organization? Is it clear and easily understood? Does it inspire others to serve for the benefit of all? Do your strengths support your mission?

5. Your Values

What are the stated values, the fundamental and deep seated priorities of your organization? Do these values directly reflect the way of life, the culture you seek to build? Do they align with your unifying message and mission?

6. A Unified Design

What do people see and hear when they walk through your organization? Is what is displayed on the walls and talked about in formal communication meetings in line with people's actual behaviors? Do you "walk your talk" or is there a disconnect, a lack of shared community, shared values, and desired behaviors?

7. Recruiting the Right People

Do you intentionally hire new people who share your organization's values and who will be effective role models for your unifying message of servant leadership?

8. Growing Servant Leaders

Do the present senior leaders of your organization live your values in everyday action? In what ways? Do they hold themselves accountable to the unifying message and underlying philosophy? Are they committed to being role models and to continual learning and improvement? Do they actively mentor and coach mid-level managers and supervisors?

9. Your Investment in Education and Training

What level of investment are you making or will you make to educate and train your people in servant leadership? In what ways could all your training programs be aligned with the principles of servant leadership? What do you need to do to improve your organization's commitment to education and training for all your people?

10. Your Assessment

Place a check mark where you believe that a more intentional design would increase the momentum of building the servant leadership culture you want.

❑ Confirming my own role as cultural architect.

❑ Identifying and implementing a few key changes this year that would increase the momentum of change this year.

❑ Defining the way of life we will commit to and communicating a unifying message that others will be inspired to embrace.

❑ Improving accountability to our values.

❑ Assuring that key leaders are servant leader role models who are committed to their own and others' continual growth and development.

❑ Hiring people who are aligned with our values and who will be effective role models.

❑ Strengthening our commitment to education and training.

11. Your Summary

Based on this chapter's Table Talk, what next steps will you take to strengthen your commitment to building a servant leadership culture?

6

Cultivating a Servant Leadership Culture

Servant leadership is about getting people to a higher level by leading people at a higher level.

—Ken Blanchard, Ph.D.

Dr. Clotaire Rapaille is an internationally respected cultural anthropologist who has spent the last thirty years identifying some of the world's most controversial culture-defining archetypes. Fortune 100 companies have paid Dr. Rapaille huge consulting fees to help them understand the reasons people buy particular products over others. He expertly discerns the various culture codes in society on such subjects as sex, money, and health. His bestselling book, *Culture Codes,* is a captivating read.[1]

Dr. Rapaille noted that Americans have a consistent habit of turning successful business leaders into celebrities. Jack Welch, Lee Iacocca, Bill Gates, and Donald Trump have reached the mega-star status equal to basketball star Michael Jordan or even movie star Brad Pitt. Rapaille is right.

Work means a great deal to us in the United States. The question "What do you do?" asked at a dinner party often means "What is your purpose in life?" I remember listening to a disgruntled executive, soon after his firing, desperately cry, "They took my life away!" To him, losing his job meant losing his identity.

If employees feel that their work provides meaning and establishes their identity in life, then where does money fit in? According to the Society of Human Resource Management,[2] the five most important aspects of employee job satisfaction are, in order:

1. Job security
2. Benefits
3. Compensation/pay
4. Opportunities to use skills and abilities
5. Feeling safe in the work environment

In other words, money certainly plays a role in employee job satisfaction. However, the surveys indicate that it is not their primary motivator. Money, in the American culture code, is simply proof of success.[3] In addition, money also verifies an employee's goodness as a person. That is why Americans give higher percentages of their earnings to charities than any other nation in the world.

JOB SATISFACTION

Tom W. Smith is a globally acknowledged expert in survey research at the University of Chicago. Author of more than 450 scholarly papers, Tom has invested his professional life into understanding how culture works in America. In an academic paper released by the University's National Opinion Research Center, Smith listed the jobs with highest and lowest job satisfaction in the United States.[4]

From the results of the survey, the least satisfying dozen jobs are primarily low-skill, manual, and service occupations, especially involving customer service and food/beverage preparation. For example, roofers had the least job satisfaction. In another category measuring happiness, the unskilled manual and service positions are the least contented.

By only looking at the least job satisfaction survey, one might conclude that money is the definitive mark for satisfaction and happiness. However, the three occupations in the top dozen on both job satisfaction and general happiness do not rank high on the salary scale. Clergy ranks first in job satisfaction and general happiness. Firefighters rank third in job satisfaction and second on general happiness, and special education teachers are the third doubly top-ranked occupation. The reason for this high job satisfaction and general happiness is not money, but the feeling of being appreciated and respected for their service. All three of these occupations instill a personal feeling of worth because these people work on behalf of others. Working to benefit others is the core idea of servant leadership.

Then why are minimal-skill, manual, and service occupations, especially customer service and food preparation occupations, low in job satisfaction and vocational happiness? The dissatisfaction likely comes from three sources: minimal personal commitment, unhealthy social climate, and authoritarian leadership culture.

- Minimal personal commitment: A positive attitude is a key difference between success and failure as an employee. Attitude affects outcome and is the necessary building block for job satisfaction and personal happiness. An undersized commitment to a task often reflects a poor attitude.

- Unhealthy social climate: A working environment that sees employees as servants without dignity will produce the conditions where customers also see service by employees as utilitarian. The unhealthy social climate diminishes the quantity and quality of service. As a result, it diminishes job satisfaction.

- Authoritarian leadership culture: Demanding, controlling, and strict leadership creates a power over people, instead of a power *with* the people for collaborative goals. This kind of leadership is based more on fear than on trust, thus creating more rules and regulations and less job satisfaction.

In other words, these occupations lack a culture of servant leadership. Servant leaders provide for the greatest number of employees to feel valued and valuable in their organization. However, cultivating a servant leadership culture is a difficult task.

What Are the Steps Necessary for Transforming an Organization's Culture?

In order to help you through the process of cultivating a servant leadership culture, this chapter is divided into three sections: the four components of transformation, the primary teaching methods for each stage of transformation, and the signposts of successful transformation.

THE FOUR COMPONENTS OF TRANSFORMATION

The four significant parts necessary for cultivating transformation within an organization are cultural architect, commitment level, climate control, and culture formation.

The following chart illustrates these parts.

Cultural Architect

In Chapter 5 we looked at the importance of a cultural architect. The cultural architect is the person with the highest level of positional power within the corporate circle of influence. This person may be the chief executive officer, the general manager of a larger organization, or even, in some cases, the human resources executive. The cultural architect must be invested professionally and personally as a servant leader. As John

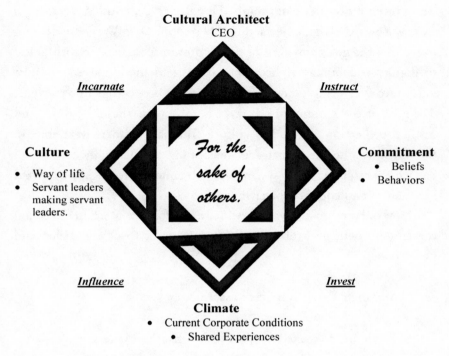

Figure 1. The Four Components of Transformation

Maxwell so eloquently puts it, the "law of the lid in leadership" is that the people will never rise higher than their leader.[5]

Commitment Level

Commitment level is the second significant component for transformation. The cultural architect must have a personal commitment of belief and behavior, values, and vocational activities that align with servant leadership. However, a high level of commitment on the part of the cultural architect is not enough. He or she must work to make everyone in the organization more committed to the principles of servant leadership. Some insightful ideas about how to do this come from an unusual source, the Communist Party. In the early 1960s, a small booklet was written by former Communist Douglas Hyde, entitled, *Dedication and Leadership*.[6] Hyde, as news editor of London's *Daily Worker*, had begun to see that the goals and aims of the Communist Party were antithetical to dignity and human rights. However, the methods the Communist Party used for recruitment to a new way of life were compelling to Hyde. The goal of the Communist Party was to remove the old culture and instill a dedication to the new culture. The party leaders were able, in the midst of a hostile climate, to successfully recruit highly committed participants to their belief system and subsequently to engage in shared experiences and common behaviors.

How did they do it? Hyde identified a fourfold approach to increasing the commitment level of an individual in order to change belief and behaviors:

- Stimulate the willingness to sacrifice and serve

- Be willing to make big demands to ensure a big response

- Provide inspirational instruction with relevant applications

- Incorporate comprehensive renovation techniques

The stimulation for service comes from a dream for something better, a vision of something great. That stimulation for service was seen in the marches and messages of Martin Luther King, Jr. during the civil rights movement. King's "I Have a Dream" speech and his "Letter from a Birmingham Jail" still evoke an emotional response for people of all colors to make a difference through sacrifice and service.[7] Stimulating the willingness comes when the heart is touched, the dream is provided, and the possibilities are explored. This stimulation for service comes when people believe that they can change the world right now by their personal impact.

The willingness to make big demands is necessary to ensure a big response. Most corporations expect little so they receive little. Then when corporations do make big demands, they focus on the wrong demands—those that are clearly self-serving and only succeed in de-motivating employees. For example, increasing work time, reducing compensation, or threatening unemployment are not incentives.

Big demands can be made when the employee sees lives improved, lives changed, or even lives saved. For example, Datron World Communications, Inc. is in the business of making military, firefighters, and police radio communications systems. If employees only see their role as producing a radio, instead of being instrumental in providing a life-saving device, they will be less committed to the task assigned. The product needs to be connected to people. Once people see and hear how their products make a difference in the world, big demands can be made.

Inspirational instruction comes through transparent instructors. These teachers don't have to be stars with their pedagogical skills, but they do have to be willing to show their scars. They have to be willing to identify with the learners because they are life-long learners themselves. They have to be willing to share how servant leadership changed the way they view employees and business plans. The novices need to see that this way of life is not only true in concept but real for the company in daily activities.

Finally, the comprehensive renovation techniques involve all the senses. Most organizations post a mission statement on the wall and stop there. However, this provides a minimal impact at best. Film, artwork, laughter, community gatherings, meals, conferences, mountain-top experiences, newsletters, emails, arrangement of furniture, smiles, and constant positive reinforcement concerning servant leadership help reinforce a different environment for your employees that involves all their senses.

Climate Control

In addition to a cultural architect and commitment, transformation requires controlling an organization's climate. Throughout the course of history, human beings through religious rituals, magical formulas, and scientific experiments have tried to alter atmospheric conditions. Climate control methods were described in Greek mythology, ancient Rome, and even the wild, wild, west in the nineteenth century. The modern era witnessed climate control methods by scientists as early as the 1940s. Today, the atmospheric phenomena of clouds, rain, snow, hail, lightning, thunderstorms, tornadoes, hurricanes, and cyclones can be altered to some degree to modify the weather conditions on a local or regional scale.[8]

Like the atmospheric conditions outside, there are atmospheric conditions inside an organization. Often you can walk into a lobby or down the corridor within a corporation and know if the corporate climate is sunny, cloudy, or raining emotionally. How is corporate climate measured? How do you modify the current corporate atmosphere?

UNDERSTANDING CORPORATE CLIMATE

Corporate climate, like weather climate, is measured over the long term. But, like the weather, people often only recognize the immediate changes. The process for making snow may take several days in the atmosphere, but people only put on their snow jackets when it begins to fall on them. In similar fashion, a corporate climate change can happen immediately: an angry interchange, a bold-faced lie concerning a project, a down-in-the-dumps attitude, or blame used to justify a late deliverable. However, those immediate signs of bad weather in corporate climate were in reality developing for weeks, months, or even years.

To understand corporate climate, it's useful to apply the terms used to measure long-term weather conditions; they are very similar to measuring long-term corporate climate. Both systems are based on several significant factors: temperature, precipitation, wind, aerosols, and insolation.[9]

- Temperature: This is the most basic indicator of climate. Like weather conditions, corporate temperatures can fluctuate during the year. You need to look at the extremes as well as the average temperature of the company. How widespread is the current heat wave within the organization? Is the lack of friendliness in the organization from the receptionist to the human resource director a sign of temporary pressure, or is it a long-term cooling trend that will signal that the company is closing in on an ice age? Levels of profanity, short fuses among executives, conflict among the workforce, and increased charges of unfair treatment are all indicators of temperature levels.

- Precipitation: Corporate precipitation is usually the level of outside business of the organization. What is the amount of rainfall your company is experiencing in terms of excessive monsoon rains (heavy workload, constant overtime) or droughts (sales down)? Rain is healthy, but if the environment cannot handle the amount of rain, destructive flooding can occur in the worksite.

- Wind: Wind is measured by speed and direction. Wind can generate powerful storms such as blizzards, tornadoes, and hurricanes. Winds may not be the same at the surface as they are at a higher elevation. This also holds true in corporate climate. Executives may experience the jet stream of high altitude wind, while at the surface the assembly line doesn't understand the pressure. A great fluctuation of speed within departments can negatively affect corporate climate.

- Aerosols: Tiny particles suspended in the air are called aerosols. They can be dust from deserts, soot from forest fires, or even pollen. Aerosols influence the amount of incoming sunlight. In the workforce, aerosols are negative, complaining, unhappy, and unproductive people. Their attitude will affect the corporate climate.

- Insolation: The amount of energy received by a piece of land from sunlight can influence its climate. In an organization, if the focus (good or bad) is always upon one department, the insolation can affect the climate of the organization.

Corporate climate needs to be assessed by the cultural architect. Modifying the corporate climate is a difficult process, but it can be done. Cloud seeding in strategic places with the right kind of people who reflect servant leadership will affect the climate. Creating an atmosphere of balance with opportunities and resources will steady the wind. Eliminating or significantly reducing the aerosols within the company will create a sunnier disposition for the workforce.

CULTURE FORMATION

Culture formation is the fourth component of transformation to a servant leadership culture. It is based upon new experiences repeated and reinforced through modeling, teaching, affirming, and rewarding. The goal is transformation of people and business. That is, changing the leadership and the workforce from a power model to a service model. The goal is to build within everyone, regardless of position, a belief and behavior that is consistent with servant leadership. The culture formation has reached its goal when the organization believes it exists for the sake of others and behaves in accordance with dignity and excellence.

TEACHING TRANSFORMATION

It is important to look at the definition of culture again before we consider the necessary teaching tools for conversion. *Corporate culture is a way of life cultivated over time through shared experiences, common behaviors, and beliefs.*

Because corporate culture is a way of life, how you teach this new lifestyle is crucial to overcoming the challenges related to the past experiences in the workforce. Because most corporations have taught that profitability is the sole purpose of the organization, the workforce has lost its faith in business and in people. They have lost the confidence that leaders have their best interests in mind when considering corporate decisions that affect the bottom line. They have lost trust. I don't blame them. Over the last twenty years in various boardrooms around the country, I have seen executives choose to receive their year-end bonuses over keeping employees on the payroll.

Because of this reality, employees experience a wide range of trust and belief when an organization commits to servant leadership. The levels are:

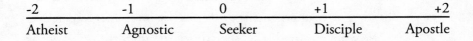

-2	-1	0	+1	+2
Atheist	Agnostic	Seeker	Disciple	Apostle

Figure 2. Commitment Levels to the Principles of Servant Leadership

1. Atheist: These people firmly believe servant leadership is simply another ploy by leadership to manipulate people for their own gain. They are generally angry and have been deeply wounded by past work experiences.

2. Agnostic: These people do not know whether servant leadership will truly work or not. Like the atheists, they have seen the ugly underbelly of corporate America and have been hurt. But unlike the atheists, they are willing to explore the benefits of servant leadership, at least out of curiosity.

3. Seeker: These people know that the current systems of leadership do not work, and they want something that provides personal fulfillment in work. They believe that servant leadership is true in concept, but they want to see if it is real in application.

4. Disciple: They are no longer exploring. They are now practicing and following the principles of servant leadership. They are in a process of lifelong learning, moving three steps forward and two steps back in this journey. They have moved from willfulness to willingness to learn and grow. Others have begun to see changes in their management style and their demeanor. They see that the disciples are actually having fun with their work and their relationship with others.

5. Apostle: These people have reached a stage where their walk and talk are nearly congruent. They seek to become better leaders and believe wholeheartedly that servant leadership is the only way to develop corporate culture. Others are drawn to them because of their consistency, calmness, and clarity of values. They are able to teach servant leadership to others, and people seek them out.

These five levels are a continuum. The teaching methods for transformation depend on what level the organization is on. Teaching servant leadership progresses through four stages.

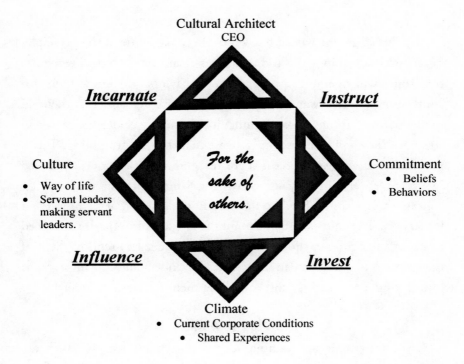

Cultural Architect
CEO

Incarnate *Instruct*

Culture
- Way of life
- Servant leaders making servant leaders.

For the sake of others.

Commitment
- Beliefs
- Behaviors

Influence *Invest*

Climate
- Current Corporate Conditions
- Shared Experiences

First Stage: Instruct

At this stage, the workforce does not know what it does not know. This is a time of solid instruction on the principles of servant leadership. Direction and clarity are important in this stage. Modeling the principles is essential. Lay out completely the beliefs and the behaviors expected within the organization. Teach, teach, and teach. Do not expect the workforce to be compliant right away with these principles. If they are like most workforces, nearly all of them will be atheists or agnostics of servant leadership. They want to see if this is just a short-term program or a lifetime investment. They want to see if there is accountability or just another training class to attend.

Second Stage: Invest

By this stage, the workforce will begin to use some of the principles of servant leadership with varying degrees of success. They will recognize that some will openly resist their new behaviors and mock them for conforming to a new way of corporate life. They will realize that their old nature of doing things makes it difficult to naturally change. So they will struggle. They will be consciously aware that they are stumbling. This is the stage where the workforce is at greatest peril. They are not experienced in servant leadership. They are receiving very little enthusiasm from their colleagues. And quite frankly, they are not very good at being servant leaders yet. The cultural architect and the already committed team need to invest their time in those individuals. They need to remind them of the vision. It is at this time the servant leader understands the importance of inspiring, encouraging, and equipping them for servant leadership.

Third Stage: Influence

By now people are gaining success as servant leaders. They are becoming disciples. The workforce is beginning to see the benefit of this way of living within their work and home. The cultural architect sees that they are becoming more competent and have regained their enthusiasm about servant leadership. The workforce is willing to talk about it and is now practicing some of the principles.

This is the time that you move from high instructive engagement to high discussion and consensus building. The cultural architect provides opportunities for interactive sessions designed so the workforce can take ownership in the learning process. Asking the right questions about servant leadership is more important at this stage than providing all the answers. In other words, the cultural architect has moved from instructor to mentor.

Fourth Stage: Incarnate

The workforce has now moved from atheist to agnostic to seeker to disciple to apostle. Very little direction is needed because they are now providing information to others. The cultural architect is there to serve as a model for all, a mentor of some selected ones, and a consistent messenger of the vision for the company. In essence, the cultural architect is developing other cultural architects within the organization. In other words, the servant leader is building other servant leaders.

THE SIGNPOSTS OF TRANSFORMATIONAL SUCCESS

Robert Greenleaf has been known as the father of modern servant leadership. In his seminal work, *Servant Leadership*, Greenleaf shares the signposts of success in his description of a servant leader. He explains, "The best test, and difficult to administer, is: do those served grow as persons; do they, while being served, become healthier, wiser, freer, more autonomous, more likely themselves to become servants? And, what is the effect on the least privileged in society; will he benefit, or, at least, will he not be further deprived?"[10]

The signposts of transformational success are:

- Choosing to serve first, aspiring to lead second

- Recognizing that your highest priority is to serve the priorities of your team

- Growing and learning, personally and professionally

- Working your business and your particular vocation for the sake of others

- Creating other servant leaders

- Making a difference in the lives least privileged

- Creating an environment of creativity, stewardship, and mentoring

Making a Positive Difference for Others

Mark Sattel is currently the manager of engineering service and one of the members of the leadership council within Datron. Mark first arrived at Datron, then known as Transworld Communication, in 1986. Even before Art Barter came on the scene at Datron, Mark was seeking another way to do business. He writes, "When I arrived in 1986, the original owner was still there as president. He cared little for his employees. He was known for his red-faced, out of control tirades ... Besides the tirades, it was clear that the quality of the product didn't matter as much as personal profits. One time he told me not to design captive hardware into a radio because of the additional 25 cents it would cost to improve the product. Another time, the president ordered radios to be buttoned up without modules knowing that the radios would be returned sometime after he sold the company."[11]

The owner's commitment was for his own personal gain, period. As owner, he created a business climate that was stormy, threatening, and unstable. His way of life produced a culture that was eventually self-destructive to the person and the products. According to Mark, the pattern continued when new leadership applied their power without a moral imperative to work for the sake of others: "The new leadership created walls of resentment between the executives. There were many open, angry arguments, with name calling and physical threats. The new president seemed to enjoy the unfolding drama between department heads. It wasn't unusual to see one department openly sabotage another department."[12]

At Datron, a series of leaders followed through the years. Some exhibited authoritative leadership, others exhibited their applied power in more hierarchal and traditional ways, but all were serving under the premise that the sole purpose of the business was financial profit. No one was interested in creating a business that would sustain profitability while enhancing personal dignity. They didn't believe it was possible to do both. Unfortunately, they created a climate and developed a culture where quarterly earnings measured success and hours worked defined commitment to the organization. In addition, a survival-of-the-fittest mentality applied to developing people, and information silos were used between departments to leverage power.

Most interactions between the employees were negative. Their behaviors, along with their beliefs, were consistent with their dysfunctional leadership. They exhibited the R.A.T. problem in corporate America:

R: Relationship Issues: The inability to get along under stressful conditions.

A: Authority Issues: Constant questioning of leadership direction and guidance. For the CEO, the authority issues can come down to a lack of trust for her executives.

T: Transition Issues: Making constant changes within the corporation and blaming others for the need of change.

According to Mark Sattel, it wasn't until Art Barter took over the leadership at Datron that he first heard of servant leadership. The past produced many scars of doubt, but Mark was also committed to being part of something greater. He states that although the transformation was difficult at times, servant leadership is gaining at Datron. Those who were unable to grasp servant leadership retreated naturally from Datron. Those remaining have developed a closeness never before witnessed at this company.

Cultivating a culture always starts with a cultural architect. Fortunately, Datron had a cultural architect and servant leader in Art Barter, who was committed to building other servant leaders.

Table Talk

Discussing and Reflecting on Chapter 6

1. Your Alignment

Do you believe that your own values, beliefs, behaviors, and key activities are in alignment with the principles and practices of servant leadership? Is it a natural fit? How would you describe your level of personal and professional investment in leading your organization as the cultural architect of a servant leadership culture?

2. Your Vision

How would you describe your vision for a better world? Did the words you wrote come from your heart? Would these words inspire and engage the hearts of others?

3. Your Company's Products/Services

In what ways does the output of your company's products and services positively impact the lives of others? Does your vision statement include the positive impact of your people's work, products, and services on others?

4. Your Big Demands

What are you asking of the people in terms of achieving your vision, your dream? What kind of commitments will be required of them over time? Will these commitments make a positive difference in their own lives and the lives of others?

5. Your Organizational Climate

By what criteria do you presently measure your organizational climate? What signs do you look for? If you could be a fly on the wall, what would you observe? What attitudes and behaviors are encouraged and allowed? What business pressures are people experiencing? How are these pressures played out in people's behaviors? Is your front line aware of the pressures and challenges? What is the gap between the attitudes and behaviors you observe and what you desire to see and experience?

6. Commitment Levels

Where would you place yourself on the continuum of commitment to the principles of servant leadership? Where would you place each person who reports directly to you? Who are your seekers, disciples, and apostles? Who are your atheists and agnostics?

7. Your Assessment

A. Check which stage best describes where you are and what you need to do to transform your culture to one of servant leadership in which all people are committed to living for the sake of others.

❏ **Stage One: Instruct**
People need direction and clarity on my vision and specific instruction on the guiding principles of servant leadership.

❏ **Stage Two: Invest**
Some people are becoming intentional as servant leaders but are struggling. They need focused support from me and other servant leaders.

❏ **Stage Three: Influence**
The workforce is beginning to see the benefit of servant leadership in both their work and home life. People are beginning to master the basic

principles of servant leadership. As cultural architect, I and other servant leaders are now using multiple forums to ensure interactive discussion. We are asking good questions to encourage people to arrive at their own answers.

❏ **Stage Four: Incarnate**

As the cultural architect, I continue to reinforce my vision and be a role model of servant leadership principles and behaviors. I and other servant leaders are actively mentoring and coaching key individuals to aid their transformation process. We are focused on helping our servant leaders build other servant leaders.

B. Based on your stage of servant leadership transformation, what specific messages or signposts of transformation do you need to reinforce in this period?

❏ Choose to serve first, aspire to lead second.

❏ Recognize that the highest priority is to serve the priorities of your team.

❏ Commit to personal growth and life-long learning, personally and professionally.

❏ Work your business and your particular vocation for the sake of others.

❏ Ensure that servant leaders are creating other servant leaders.

❏ Make a difference in the lives of the least privileged.

❏ Create an environment of creativity, stewardship, and mentoring.

8. Your Summary

Based on this chapter's reflection and discussion questions, what next steps will you take as cultural architect in leading your organization's transformational process?

7

Vision, Values, and Virtues

At this moment, America's highest economic need is higher ethical standards, upheld by responsible business leaders.
—GEORGE W. BUSH

My wife Bobbi is a great cook. I love the effort and time she puts into making a meal for our family, which is not only delicious but a delight to the eyes. Occasionally, she has trusted me to help with the preparation of the food. Since I am better at eating than cooking, I stick quite closely to the recipe, making sure I have carefully measured the right ingredients. I have learned from my wife that you can occasionally add a new spice or something extra, but the essential ingredients must remain the same if you want a delicious meal.

As it is with cooking, so it is with servant leadership. Listen to the experts, and you will see several ingredients that are necessary to develop a servant leadership culture.

Over and over, experts stress the importance of self-awareness, listening, consensus building, trust, feedback, empathy, community, and so on. The servant leadership chefs all know the essential ingredients of developing an invigorating environment and enthusiastic workforce. However, here we will concentrate on three key ingredients that are essential in a servant leadership culture: vision, values, and virtues. Each ingredient was vital for Datron as the corporation moved away from the power model of leadership to a servant model of leadership.

EMBRACING THE VISION

"Without vision, the people perish."[1] Vision is the ability to see what is invisible to others. In corporate language, vision describes the vivid mental image created by a leader so that people will have the experience of truly seeing into the future. Reading the words of some of the movers and shakers in the world can help us see the importance of vision in leadership. Vision inspires greatness, unites people, and dominates conversations. Vision is always bigger than the leader and more powerful than any one person's convictions. Vision identifies values and instills virtues, regardless of cost.

DATRON'S STORY OF VISION

The first chapter of this book describes the problem of misguided power in leadership. Through those early pages you read about Datron's history of misapplied power and an obvious lack of corporate vision. You could see the heavy price the organization and its employees had to pay for this kind of leadership. Through the leadership of Art Barter and the executive team, Datron World Communications started to embrace the vision for servant leadership. It brought clarity to every program, every product, and every person within Datron.

VISION STATEMENTS

The vision statement of Datron World Communications states the company's purpose: "a self-sustaining, profitable communications company which positively impacts the lives of others today and in the future." These words define the type of company Datron wants to be: "a self-sustaining, profitable communications company." But notice that the statement also includes the directed mission: "which positively impacts the lives of others today and in the future." The financial success of the company is necessary to achieve its real mission—making a positive difference in the lives of others. In essence, Datron's business is designed for the sake of others. The mission and purpose of Datron is the vision! Notice how different Datron's vision is compared with those of some Fortune 500 companies:[2]

> *"To combine aggressive strategic marketing with quality products and services at competitive prices to provide the best insurance value for consumers."*

> *"Profitable growth through superior customer service, innovation, quality, and commitment."*

> *"To build shareholder value by delivering pharmaceutical and health care products, services, and solutions in innovative and cost-effective ways. We will realize this mission by setting the highest standards in service, reliability, safety, and cost containment in our industry."*

> *"To be America's best run, most profitable automotive retailer."*

> *"Our mission is to provide undisputed marketplace leadership."*

There is nothing wrong with creating greater shareholder value or making a profit in your company. There is nothing wrong with increasing market share or becoming a premier provider or a global leader in your industry. In fact, these mission statements can be very beneficial. However, there is something short-sighted when a Fortune 500 company doesn't consider that its primary mission should be to exist for the sake of others, and not just for the sake of others in their exclusive shareholder family but for the sake of making this world to the least and the last a better place. The stakeholders for every company are our local, national, and global community!

To their credit, many Fortune 500 companies have special funds for helping charitable organizations with their key projects. But special funds are not enough. Unless all companies see that their primary role is not to maximize profitability but to maximize positive impact on their world, they will be driven by quarterly earnings more than changed lives. Feeding the hungry, healing the sick, educating the illiterate, building homes for the homeless, caring for the elderly, providing for the children, and helping the hurting must be the reasons for businesses to sustain profitability.

Datron exists to make a positive impact on the lives of others today and in the future. Why do Art Barter, his executive team, and the employees have such a commitment? There are two reasons: perception and perspective.

DATRON'S PERCEPTION: IN GOD WE TRUST

Perception provides discernment and insight to a vision. Datron's perception is that its mission is a calling to exist for the sake of others. Datron does not believe its calling is to be sectarian, although many of its employees worship in various denominations. Datron does not believe that its calling is to judge others from different faiths or nonfaith systems. Proselytizing to a faith system is neither required nor advocated. Those who do not have a belief in God buy into the culture at Datron because they too believe they need to make this world a better place.

DATRON'S PERSPECTIVE: IN PEOPLE WE INVEST

Perception is personal. For example, one person may notice things that are not obvious to others. Perspective, on the other hand, is how things are in reality. People who cannot perceive the importance of the belief "In God we trust" can certainly see the reality of Datron's investment in people.

Carol Malinski serves as an example. When she arrived at Datron in 1996, Carol had high hopes for her new company, but she describes how first impressions can be so wrong:

"What I thought would be a great learning experience became an exercise in frustration. What I discovered about the real Datron was a culture of holding onto the information to keep the power … My coworker was afraid to ask anyone how to do her job so she would stuff paperwork within her desk instead of entering this needed information on the computer."[3]

Today, Carol Malinski serves as a planning manager within Datron. She has seen the company change before her eyes because of a leadership committed to applying their power with a moral imperative. She believes in the motto, "In God we trust, in people we invest." She states, "Art's purchase of the company was the beginning of a new day for those of us old-timers. I am proud to come to work in a place where the lobby boldly states 'In God we trust, In People We Invest.' In this Datron, if I need assistance with something, I cannot only freely approach my direct manager; I also have a group of peers and colleagues who will gladly give me assistance."[4]

Datron World Communications invests in their employees through their extensive training and development programs that include the Servant Leadership Institute, educational reimbursements, career development opportunities, personal mentoring, and small-group coaching. Art Barter meets weekly with the executive staff, managers, and supervisors to discuss practical business issues and how they relate to the servant leadership model.

Not only does Datron invest in its employees, but the company also invests in its customer and vendor base. Whether the customer is the military, a public safety agency, or the U.S. Department of Homeland

Security, the strategy is still the same from the servant leader perspective as the company's tag line suggests: "Performance you require, value you expect."

Datron's investment extends beyond its employees, customers, and vendors to include local and worldwide agencies and communities that need resources to help them live better lives. In its 2008 fiscal year, Datron donated more than $790,000 to fifty-two nonprofit organizations in ten countries around the world. Datron walks its talk.

USING CORE VALUES TO ESTABLISH THE VISION

Vision is important. But vision can only be sustained if the leadership is committed to core values within the organization. According to Art Barter, the core values are more important to the vitality of Datron than any financial goals within the company. Five core values have been established within Datron.

Our Families Come First

All the mental health experts avow the importance of families in improving the quality of life. Despite the affirmations you receive from your colleagues, what your family thinks about you probably means more to you than anything else. Families have a way of multiplying the pleasures and lessening the pains of life. So why do companies want to negate the benefits of family by increasing their demands for more of their employees' time? Over the last five years, nearly a dozen executives in different industries have told me that they have lost their soul to their company. The companies have bought the employees' time and talents. Unfortunately, their families lose. Ultimately, due to resentment, job hunting, and deception, the companies lose as well.

Datron's core value, families come first, is placed at the top of the company's values. Datron never wants to be accused of neglecting the most important institutional structure in society by reducing parental time, hurting marriages, or ignoring family crises. As a result, Datron frowns on weekend work and excessive hours during the week.

Honor and Serve Others

Datron believes that every individual, regardless of his or her role within the company, is to be esteemed. Because of that respect for one another, we will not soil someone's reputation through gossip. In fact, honoring an individual means to treat that person as a man or woman of distinction. This value says to all employees that it is a great privilege to work together in order to make a positive difference in this world. And because we honor others, we serve them.

Conduct Ourselves Ethically and with Integrity

Conducting ourselves ethically means more than conducting ourselves within legal limits. It means that regardless of the circumstances, the employees at Datron will serve without hidden agendas and will not misrepresent themselves or their products. They will do what is agreed on in the time to which it was agreed. Professionally and personally, they will be people of integrity. They will be people who have the courage to do the right thing.

Be Honest and Trustworthy

All these core values are built on trust. Genuine teamwork is built on trust, and trust is built on truth. Every firefighter knows the importance of trust. Their very lives are at stake if someone does not have their back in providing the support needed. Every Marine that shouts *semper fi* knows that fellowship as a Marine is built on trust. You cannot go into battle without trusting your partners. Even in NASCAR, the pit crew works together so efficiently because their teamwork is built on trust. Being honest and trustworthy demands a person of character, competency, and contribution. In one of the best books on leadership, *The Speed of Trust*, Stephen M.R. Covey describes what is necessary to be a trustworthy person. He writes, "Trust is a function of two things: character and competence. Character includes your integrity, your motive, and your intent with people. Competence includes your capabilities, your skills, your results, and your track record. And both are vital."[5]

I believe the third factor necessary to have credibility before others is contribution. The biblical term for contribution is sacrifice. The contemporary term would be the willingness to give away. A contribution is the willingness to give away what you value so that you can play a role in achieving something beneficial for the sake of others. But contributions should not be limited to philanthropy alone, because contribution is more than just money. Contribution means that you are taking your rightful and active role in being a citizen of the world. Contribution truly involves time, talent, and treasure!

Be Uncompromising in Our Values

Since Datron believes values provide the foundation for the vision, we cannot compromise them. Just as strong foundations must be built to support architectural structures, Datron needs an uncompromising commitment to its values. Within Datron, it is everyone's responsibility to be a servant leader. Servant leadership is not an elective course in management development. It is a way of life, a lifestyle. Therefore, everyone is required to be uncompromising with the organization's values: families come first, honor and serve others, conduct ourselves ethically and with integrity, and never forget to be honest and trustworthy.

Datron recognizes the imperfections of humanity. We will stumble, but we must always get up. With these values as our foundation, we can embrace the clarity of vision.

USING CARDINAL VIRTUES TO ENERGIZE THE VISION

Virtue is the health of the soul of the corporation. Embracing a clear vision provides purpose and meaning to a corporation. Building core values provides the necessary foundation for the vision. But what gives life to the vision and columns to the foundation are the *cardinal* virtues.

Plato first formulated these four universal laws of moral living: wisdom, justice, courage, and moderation.[6] The ancient use of the word cardinal comes from the Latin *cardo,* which means a hinge, that on which a thing turns, its principal point. In modern day language, the word *cardinal* means basic, fundamental, or prime. These virtues provide vitality for people and the institutions they serve. All other virtues hinge on these four.

- Wisdom: Initially this virtue was called prudence. It is putting reasonable action into practice with regard to appropriateness of the context. Wisdom is knowledge applied correctly. Plato calls wisdom the "chief and leader of all virtues."[7]

- Justice: This virtue involves the proper judgment and subsequent action regarding human rights, interests, and fairness. Justice provides life to individuals and societies. Injustice destroys people and deconstructs institutions.

- Moderation: Initially called temperance, this virtue describes the practice of self-control and moderation both bodily and emotionally. Moderation is not cowardly or dull, suppressive or repressive. Moderation actually provides life. Immoderate appetites lead to greed, the modern day crisis for corporations and individuals.

- Courage: This cardinal virtue is listed last not because it is considered the least, but because it is needed the most by corporations, society, and individuals. Alexander Solzhenitsyn, the Russian novelist who was awarded the Nobel Prize in

Literature and the Templeton Prize, suffered greatly for
his commitment to truth, liberation, and freedom for all.
Imprisoned for many years by the Soviet Union for his writings,
Solzhenitsyn spoke eloquently as a freed man when he addressed
the future leaders at Harvard University during commencement
exercises on June 8, 1978: "A decline in courage may be the most
striking feature which an outside observer notices in the West
in our days. The Western world has lost its civil courage, both
as a whole and separately, in each country, each government,
each political party and of course in the United Nations. Such
a decline in courage is particularly noticeable among the ruling
groups and the intellectual elite, causing an impression of loss of
courage by the entire society."[8]

Leaders need courage. Change agents cannot inspire, equip, or
encourage others without courage. All vision is fueled by courage.
Courage brings deliberate and decisive action. Courage means you are
willing to become a deep person rather than a shallow one, a discerning
person rather than an indiscriminate one.

These four cardinal virtues are not the only great virtues. They are
simply the hinge of all the other moral virtues.

Saint Thomas Aquinas in his magnum opus, *Summa Theologica*,
modified the four cardinal virtues with three additional theological
virtues: faith, hope, and love.[9]

- Faith: Trusting steadfastly the source of your belief

- Hope: An assurance of a future good that goes beyond wishing

- Love: Seeking the best on behalf of others (the most charitable
  way of living)

These seven virtues have been expressed in secular and sacred writings from ancient antiquity, yet they will always remain universal truths. In Plato's *Republic*, the four cardinal virtues reflect the nature of the soul. For example, our reason thinks. When our reason thinks well, we have wisdom. Our appetite desires. When we control our appetite (not just for food), we have moderation, which serves us and others well. Our emotions generate a variety of feelings like fear, anger, anxiety, and respect. When we manage our emotions, we have courage. In Plato's *Republic*, society mirrors the individual soul.[10]

Socrates was known for his words, "The unexamined life is not worth living."[11] Leading self before others demands purpose, perception, and perspective. It also demands a solid foundation of core values and a life defined and energized by virtues.

It is not that individuals, society, and corporations have wanted so much in life; it is that they have settled for so little. They have allowed their own greed for maximizing profitability, pursuing various forms of entertainment, and the need for personal glory to cause them to settle into a philosophy that Milton Friedman speaks of and nearly all of the Fortune 500 mission statements follow. However, the central role of a corporation is not to thrive for the sake of their shareholders. Companies exist to be a sustaining profitable organization *for the sake of others*. Their goal must be to make the world a better place where there is life, not death, blessings instead of cursing, and the least and last is provided for.

Table Talk

Discussing and Reflecting on Chapter 7

1. Embrace Your Vision

In what ways do your organization's vision and mission unite your people in the beliefs that what they do is for the sake of others and that through their work they make a positive impact on the world? In what ways could you clarify these statements to reflect doing business for the sake of others and to make the world a better place?

2. Perception and Perspective

Do you experience your vision and mission as a calling? In what ways? What is the source of your belief and faith? Is it God, the Bible, a particular faith-based system? What universal beliefs are you calling out in other people, regardless of their faith or denomination? Datron's stated belief is "In God We Trust, In People We Invest." What statement would you make that captures your core beliefs? Is this your unifying message to your organization?

3. Establish the Vision with Core Values

Values are the foundational truths, the deep-seated priorities intended to guide the organization and people's behaviors. In what ways are you communicating the importance of living these values in everyday behaviors and actions?

4. Bring It into Everyday Action

Are your organization's unifying message, vision, mission, and values in the forefront of people's thinking and conversations? Do these statements infuse business planning and serve as guideposts for business planning, communication, and decision making? Do they guide the perceptions and behaviors of your people? Is this thinking infused into all programs, products, and services? What could you do to improve the ability of all of your people to integrate these messages into everyday thinking and action?

5. Reflect on Virtues

Reflect on your defining moments and personal encounters with adversity. What virtues did you demonstrate? In what ways has your life been defined and energized by virtue? In your organization, how would you talk about identifying and recognizing virtues and using them for leading oneself?

6. Your Assessment

Check the boxes describing areas where you need to improve.

❑ Improve and clarify our vision statement so that we are united in the belief that we work for the sake of others and to make the world a better place.

❑ Articulate and communicate my own calling and the universal beliefs it represents. Craft this message into a unifying message.

❑ Describe what our core values mean to me and how I use them in guiding my everyday behaviors and actions. Ask people to engage in a similar process of personally connecting to our core values so that they understand how these values can guide their everyday actions.

❏ Improve the alignment, integration, and simplicity of our vision, mission, values, and unifying message. Educate others and demonstrate how these elements can infuse all our business planning, communication, and decision-making processes. Encourage people to put these elements into the forefront of their thinking and actions.

❏ Ask people to think about virtues and to recognize how the virtues of wisdom, justice, moderation, courage, faith, hope, and love have been demonstrated in their own lives. Ask people to reflect on how these virtues can guide and energize us as we go forward.

7. Your Summary

Based on this chapter's reflection and discussion questions, what next steps will you take to effectively lead yourself and the people of your organization?

8

Extending the Servant Leadership Culture to the Community

Planets explode; galaxies implode. We are an insignificant flake, except as we are alive and experiencing ourselves in life. And for that I say please devote your life to making a better world. Don't waste one day!

—PATCH ADAMS, M.D.

Three doctors, along with seventeen of their friends, wanted to live their lives for the sake of others. They turned a six-bedroom home into a hospital and made that hospital into a home for up to fifty overnight guests. The hospital was free, open twenty-four hours a day, seven days a week, and covered every medical problem possible. Five hundred to one thousand patients were seen every month. This hospital was the beginning of the Gesundheit Institute. These twenty pioneers of compassionate medicine had to take outside jobs to meet their financial needs, but not one staff member left in the first nine years![1]

In 1998, Universal Pictures told their moving story in a full-length film starring Robin Williams. The movie, *Patch Adams*, was based on Patch Adams's book, *Gesundheit*. It helped launch a global teaching outreach to medical and nursing schools in more than sixty-five countries.

Dr. Adams is firmly committed to social activism with a unique twist. His new project focuses on clown diplomacy in locations experiencing extreme violence. Patch Adams and his team are healing crushed human spirits worldwide. They believe that "you cannot separate the health of the individual from the health of the community and of society."[2] The Gesundheit Institute exists for the sake of others.

That kind of passion to serve can cross industry lines and international borders. Datron isn't in the medical business, but they are in the business of saving lives through radio communication. Datron also believes their company exists not only for their employees and customers, but also for the forgotten and the ignored, the hurting and the hunted, and the least and the last. Datron exists for the sake of others.

Almost immediately upon purchase of Datron, Art and Lori Barter established a charitable fund within Datron for causes that range from homelessness to disease research to school programs and ministries around the world. They secured the help of Fidelity Charitable Gift Fund to guide Datron so they could maximize their giving and direct it toward legitimate needs in the world. The Gift Fund's mission "is to further the American tradition of philanthropy by providing programs that make charitable giving simple and effective."[3]

The Barters and Datron seeded the account with a $100,000 check, and two months later they added another check for almost $500,000 to make sure the fund was on solid ground. Some of the first-year grants provided by Datron were to the Boys and Girls Club, the Leukemia and Lymphoma Society, an orphanage in Kenya, the Alpha Project for a homeless shelter, the Special Olympics, ALS Lou Gehrig's disease research, Breast Cancer Research, women's shelters, Alzheimer's disease research, AIDS research, and various missionary trips in the Global South. They provided help for the blind, the crippled, the hungry, and the hurting.[4]

EMPLOYEE PARTICIPATION AND ANONYMITY

The uniqueness of this program lies not in the dollars given, but in the total involvement of Datron's employees. Any Datron employee, regardless of position, can fill out an application requesting a grant to a charitable organization. The employee simply has to state the purpose of the gift, the reasons why this particular charitable organization is close to his or her heart, and provide its IRS-issued ID number. Every month, the charitable fund committee within Datron reads the requests, assesses the viability along with the needs of the receiving organization, and if approved, has Fidelity send them a check. Employees are deeply touched that the work they do at Datron can make a difference in the lives of others, sometimes even their own family members.

For example, Letty Alaniz Edwards is an administrative assistant at Datron. Her sixteen-year-old brother, Anthony, had the energy you would expect of a teenager. Anthony loved playing video games and spending time with his nieces and nephews. He was such a wonderful kid that he didn't even mind receiving a kiss occasionally from his big sister. His family was proud of him.

But in December 2006, Anthony began to complain about pain around his left knee. The pain became stronger, so his parents took Anthony to a pediatrician in March 2007. Prescribing an anti-inflammatory, the doctor arranged for Anthony to get blood tests to investigate further. A few days later, still awaiting the results of the blood tests, Anthony was running in physical education class and broke his left femur. The femur, the thigh bone, is the longest, largest, and one of the strongest bones in the body. When Anthony was taken to the hospital, the doctors confirmed his parents' worst fears.

Anthony was diagnosed with osteosarcoma, a common type of bone cancer among children, adolescents, and young adults. Because of the severity of the break and the advanced nature of the cancer, Anthony was moved from Hemet Hospital, close to his home, to the Children's Hospital of Orange County (CHOC) in the city of Orange, California.[5]

After he had been in the hospital for three months, the doctors decided that the only course of action to save Anthony's life was to remove his left leg. Anthony stayed an additional month at CHOC for treatment and recovery. Then he received chemotherapy and stayed periodically, for days at a time, at CHOC for an additional nine months.

Letty, her parents, and her sister stayed the first three months at the nearby Ronald McDonald House so they could spend every possible moment with Anthony. After four months, they started rotating, with each person spending two days at a time at the Ronald McDonald House so they could be with Anthony during chemotherapy. Every night, meals were provided to them by volunteer cooks, and they had a quiet place to sleep.

Needless to say, the family was grateful for the generous hospitality provided by the Ronald McDonald House. Letty was happy that Datron offered her a way to express that gratitude. As she said, "When I started working at Datron, I realized that I had an opportunity to say thank you to the Ronald McDonald House. I sent in my donation request to the Datron Charitable Committee, and they approved it. I was so happy and excited to know that this wonderful place that helped my whole family for a whole year was going to receive a donation from my place of employment. It made me so proud to work at Datron."[6]

The second part of Datron's unique way of giving is their commitment to be anonymous. The company does not want to receive public recognition for their gifts. Many times the recipient organization wants to celebrate Datron's gifts with public acknowledgments through the media or special dinners; Datron always turns these offers down. Like the biblical proverb, "But when you do a charitable deed, do not let your left hand know what your right hand is doing, that your charitable deed may be in secret; and your Father who sees in secret will Himself reward you openly."[7] Datron prefers to give without recognition.

Extending the Servant Leadership Culture to the Community

Recently, a vendor, seeing the mission of Datron lived out in generous action, recommended Art Barter to be the most admired CEO of the year in San Diego. Barter was awarded that honor but missed the dinner by arranging a business trip to the East Coast at the same time. It is not that Datron and Art aren't grateful that their gifts are appreciated; it is just not the style of this humble man or the organization he represents. Several representatives from the company accepted the award on his behalf that night.

Sheri Nasim, director of strategic and operational planning, describes her work on the Datron Charitable Committee.

> *During the three years I sat on the committee, the employees of Datron made donations of over $2.5 million to 144 nonprofit organizations around the world.*
>
> *We contributed to medical research, missions, school programs, orphanages and burn institutes. We provided food and shelter to victims of the 2007 earthquake in Lima, Peru, and to the homeless in our own downtown. We built homes for families in Tijuana and provided headstones for unclaimed orphans in San Diego. Stray animals were cared for in the Hawaiian Islands, and grown men received their first wheelchair in Ethiopia.*
>
> *The company refuses public recognition for its donations, but we are thrilled to get thank you letters and pictures from around the world. We frame each letter, photograph, and child's drawing, and hang them in a long hallway for all of our employees to see. Art refers to The Wall each quarter as he gives a financial update to all employees and recognizes how our hard work has benefited a child in Vietnam or a mission to Zimbabwe.[8]*

MONEY AND VALUES

How we spend our money and how we give our money is a moral document of what we truly believe. Martin Luther, the great religious reformer in the sixteenth century, once wrote, "The last part of a person to be converted is his wallet." In the presidential election of 2008, much of the dialogue between the Democratic and Republican candidates for president and vice president centered on the idea of sacrifice. I wondered whether our nation's leaders were living out their words personally in their own sacrificial giving. What I found out is that Martin Luther's quote was not only relevant to the sixteenth century, the reformer's quote was also relevant to our twenty-first century leaders.

Vice President Joe Biden said, "Do not tell me what you value. Show me your budget and I will tell you what you value."[9] However, according to the *Chronicle of Philanthropy*, Biden and his wife, Jill, have given an average of $369 per year to charities in the past decade, as shown on their tax returns. Their income for 2007 was nearly $320,000. President Barack Obama and his wife, Michelle, have increased their charitable giving percentage every year since 2000. The first five years the average giving was only 1 percent of their $200,000 annual income. In 2007, with nearly $1 million in income, his campaign indicated that they were giving 6 percent to charitable organizations.[10]

If you are thinking that I am only picking on the two winners in the presidential race, I am not. My point is not about political agendas, but about living for the sake of others which includes your time, talents, and *treasures*. Former Governor Sarah Palin's record of giving is a little lower than the American public average of 2.2 percent.[11] Senator John McCain's records indicate that a robust 26 percent of his annual gross income was given to charities. However, Senator McCain did not include his wife's annual income of $6 million, so we do not know the exact percentage of charitable giving.[12]

Although Americans are the largest contributors to charities of all other nations in amount and percentages, most of us still fall short on the ancient concept of tithing to help others.

TITHING FOR THE SAKE OF OTHERS

The word tithe means one-tenth. Tithing was an ancient practice among many religions and world cultures. Before the Jewish Law was instituted concerning the tithe, the Old Testament spoke of Abraham and Jacob giving a tenth of all they owned in gratitude for the blessings of God (Gen. 14:18–20; Gen. 28:20–22). In the New Testament, the early Christians gave generously and joyfully for the sake of others to demonstrate love toward God and one another (Acts 4:32–35; 2 Cor. 9:7).

Very early on, Datron World Communications, Inc. and the Barter family decided that they would give a tithe of the profits of the company for the sake of others. Datron's Charitable Fund corporate policy allocates the use of the funds four ways:[13]

- 40 percent will be set aside for the sake of worldwide and local community projects and programs

- 40 percent will be set aside for the sake of worldwide and local ministry projects and programs, regardless of faith orientation

- 10 percent will be set aside for the sake of the Barters' home church

- 10 percent will be set aside for future needs and will not be available for distribution for a period of twelve months

STORIES OF CHANGED HEARTS AND IMPROVED LIVES

Lives have been changed in dramatic ways because of the financial generosity of Datron. I have interviewed scores of employees within Datron about the Charitable Fund. Many leave my office in tears. All feel a sense of gratitude to Datron for their kindness and tenderness. Letters of thanks from the recipients are available on Datron's intranet for all the employees to read and to smile and weep over. In the hallways, the walls tell the stories of changed lives in the same way a cathedral's stained glass tells the biblical stories of love and redemption. Of the many stories, these two stand out for me.

Sarah Nguyen and the Voice of Love

In 1969, the My Lai massacre became public, the first draft lottery since World War II was held, and three hundred students at Harvard University seized the administration building in protest of the war. By year's end 40,024 Americans had been killed since this conflict started.[14] It was that very same year that Sarah Nguyen was born in Viet Nam. During her childhood and adolescence, Sarah saw people treated worse than animals.

In 1991, at the age of twenty-two, Sarah came to the United States. Sarah was a university graduate in Viet Nam, and she wanted to continue her studies in the United States. But her commitment to her family back home propelled her to the workforce instead of the classroom. Holding different jobs over the years, Sarah eventually married and became a mother of two girls. In 2005, she started at Datron as a senior manufacturing engineer.

She wrote recently telling me how a visit to her homeland left her with a strong desire to help people there. "Many questions came to me, as I did not know anyone out there and how I could start. After months of searching, I found the Voice of Love Foundation. I felt connected when I heard the true story from the founder of VOL, who had exactly the same thought as me about helping my hurting people."

The next step was to approach the Datron Charitable Fund: "When I realized that Datron had a charitable program, my hope to help others in my homeland was even bigger. To me, Datron's Charitable Fund is a gift of love. I could not control my tears when I first heard that my fund request was approved. I knew right away that my wish came true … I now understand why the Barters and Datron care so passionately about others."[15]

Every act of compassion makes a difference. It makes a difference to the people we help, and it makes a difference in our own lives.

Free Wheelchair Mission

Free Wheelchair Mission is an international nonprofit organization dedicated to providing inexpensive but durable wheelchairs for impoverished disabled people in developing nations. For most of them, a wheelchair is a dream far beyond their wildest expectation. The organization has sent hundreds of thousands of wheelchairs, providing people with dignity, autonomy, and mobility. The cost to make, ship, and deliver is less than $50 per wheelchair. Here is a note we received by one of the missionaries that distributed the wheelchairs on our behalf:[16] "Thank you so much for Datron's contribution to the Free Wheelchair Mission. It is hard for me to describe what an impact that will make. When I was in Ethiopia in November, I saw people dragging themselves along the ground or being carried from twenty-five kilometers away by their entire village. One man said that he had been to the district headquarters five times before when he heard there would be wheelchairs, only to find it untrue. He left with his first wheelchair."

Inspiring stories like these show that Datron understands that they can make a difference in the world. The executives and the employees understand that every radio system built is designed to help the customers save lives through effective communication. But they also know that the profits of their work will be used to help others in our local, national, and worldwide community.

Dr. Patch Adams has probably never heard of Datron World Communications or their commitment to servant leadership. Most of the employees within Datron have never heard of Gesundheit Institute. But Art Barter and Patch Adams, and Datron and Gesundheit Institute, have something in common: Their leader is committed to servant leadership, and their organization exists for the sake of others. May their tribe increase in a world that is suffering from the greed and self-interest of leaders so that the deeply hurting, confused, and unenlightened can truly be helped.

Table Talk

Discussing and Reflecting on Chapter 8

1. For the Sake of Others

Does your organization have a commitment to those less fortunate? Is charitable giving an important part of your organization's intention? Is the focus of your corporate giving local, national, or global? Describe the mission or purpose of the gifts you make. If charitable giving has not been on your agenda in the past, comment on what you envision going forward, in terms of making a commitment to people in need.

2. Awareness

How aware are your people of the need to serve the larger community that exists beyond your organization? Do you integrate this topic into your formal and informal communication with employees?

3. Stories

In what ways do you capture the stories of people who have benefited from your charitable giving? Do you share these stories with your employees? If not, how could you improve your organization's capacity to understand its impact on serving the needs of those less fortunate?

4. Employee Involvement

Do your employees have an opportunity to directly participate in the organization's commitment to serve the less fortunate? In what ways?

5. Your Summary

What next steps will you take to improve your intention, commitment, and contribution to people less fortunate and in need of your help?

Epilogue

From my windowed office, I have been watching workers construct a new office building. First, they graded the ground and carefully laid out the foundation. Once the foundation was completed, the concrete walls were up in less than two weeks.

Servant leadership must be developed in much the same way as a contractor would construct a building. In order to create a proper foundation, we need to identify the imperfections in the soil that have hurt the organization in the past. The fundamental problem within organizations today is applied power without a moral imperative. As a result, organizations are committed to the lowest measure of success in justifying their existence: money. Leadership is driven by the short-term financial goals and reduces the dignity of every human being to a simple measure of efficiency. Labor is no longer an asset. Instead, it is an expense to reduce. Without the moral imperative that all organizations should exist for the sake of others, leadership is driven by self-serving goals and narcissistic means. This kind of power leaves a permanent, pervasive, and personal stress that prohibits creativity, hinders redemptive work, and eliminates genuine transformation of the organization's people.

Once the ground has been tilled to create the right kind of soil, a foundation has to be created that is structurally sound, flexible in application, and innovative in design. An epiphany is needed. These defining moments have great significance in the life of an executive. They provide opportunities for leaders to gain clarity about their calling and their role in contributing for the sake of others. They also teach leaders that we must lead ourselves before we can lead others.

The formation of a new kind of leader initially exists in the context of adversity. But the adversity will reveal the character of the leader and show others that he or she is truly a servant leader.

The ground has been tilled, the foundation has been laid. Next, the walls of the organization can be constructed in a manner that will equip, inspire, and encourage people to do their work for the sake of others. Defining a corporate culture over time through shared experiences, common behaviors, and beliefs necessitates a cultural architect who is the primary leader of the organization. The process of cultivating a servant leadership culture calls for the cultural architect to have a steadfast commitment to certain beliefs and behaviors that dignify people, create a new climate through positive, shared experiences, and equip others to become servant leaders. The essentials of a servant leadership culture will be evident by the way employees embrace the vision, live out the core values, and relearn key virtues.

Finally, the servant-led organization is completed with the knowledge that the financial bottom line is not the essential bottom line. It is the employees who determine a company's success or failure. The servant leader extends the servant leadership culture to the community because organizations exist not for their shareholders, or for their exclusive stakeholders, but for the world. It is the forgotten, the ignored, the least, and the last, the hunted, and the hurting that must be helped as much as the stockholder, shareholder, or even stake-holder.

This is a book about creating a servant leadership culture and building servant leaders. But the principles discussed in these pages would only be theoretical without the illustrations of the transformation of the lives at Datron and its leader, Art Barter. Art Barter changed because he recognized the timelessness of the message of servant leadership and how it is greatly needed in corporate America today. He needed to change his leadership style to truly be alive and fully engaged in the world around him. In four years, Art took a company nearly destroyed by corporate greed to one that is focused on its higher purpose—positively impacting the lives of others, today and in the future.

But this story is merely a tale unless you take stock of your own work and ask yourself if you are contributing to an organization that recognizes its higher purpose. Whether you are a sole practitioner or an employee of a multinational conglomerate, you have influence; you have gifts. I hope that you will use this book to examine the impact you are making. At the end of the day, have your gifts and talents been used to line shareholder pockets or have you left the world incrementally better by applying your talent to help others?

Appendix

A Library for Servant Leaders

The Art of Servant Leadership: Designing Your Organization for the Sake of Others
Tony Baron

The Cross and the Towel: Aligning Your Church to His Church
Tony Baron

Leaders
Warren Bennis and Burt Nanus

Servant Leader
Ken Blanchard

Lead like Jesus: Lessons from the Greatest Leadership Role Model of All Time
Ken Blanchard and Phil Hodges

Leading at a Higher Level: Blanchard on Leadership and Creating High Performing Organizations
Ken Blanchard

The Heart of a Leader: Insights on the Art of Influence
Ken Blanchard

Appendix: A Library for Servant Leaders

Whale Done!: The Power of Positive Relationships
Ken Blanchard, Thad Lacinak, Chuck Tompkins, and Jim Ballard

Built to Last
Jim Collins and Jerry Porras

Good to Great
Jim Collins

The Speed of Trust: The One Thing That Changes Everything
Stephen M. R. Covey

The 7 Habits of Highly Effective People
Stephen R. Covey

Principle-Centered Leadership
Stephen R. Covey

The Eighth Habit: From Effectiveness to Greatness
Stephen R. Covey

Leadership Is an Art
Max Dupree

Leadership Jazz
Max Dupree

Leading without Power: Finding Hope in Serving Community
Max Dupree

Robert K. Greenleaf: A Life of Servant Leadership
Don M. Frick, Larry C. Spears, and Peter M. Senge

Appendix: A Library for Servant Leaders

The Power of Servant Leadership
Robert K. Greenleaf, Larry C. Spears, and Peter B. Vaill

Servant Leadership: A Journey into the Nature of Legitimate Power and Greatness
Robert K. Greenleaf, Larry C. Spears, and Stephen R. Covey

The Leadership Challenge
James M. Kouzes and Barry S. Posner

Developing the Leader within You
John C. Maxwell

The 21 Irrefutable Laws of Leadership
John C. Maxwell

Today Matters
John C. Maxwell

Winning with People
John C. Maxwell

Talent Is Never Enough
John C. Maxwell

Maxwell Leadership Bible
John C. Maxwell

Martin Luther King, Jr. on Leadership
Donald T. Phillips

Appendix: A Library for Servant Leaders

Lincoln on Leadership
Donald T. Phillips

The Purpose-Driven Life
Rick Warren

Endnotes

Foreword

1. John C. Maxwell, *Put Your Dream to the Test: 10 Questions That Will Help You See It and Seize It* (Nashville, TN: Thomas Nelson, 2009), 128.

Introduction

1. John Zenger and Joseph Folkman, *The Inspiring Leader: Unlocking the Secrets of How Extraordinary Leaders Motivate,* 1st ed. (New York: McGraw-Hill, 2009).

Chapter 1

1. Gene W. Ray, Ph.D., interviewed by University of Tennessee Physics Newsletter, *Cross Sections*, Knoxville, TN, Spring/Summer 2002 Issue.
2. Mike Allen, "Titan Buys Datron. (Titan Corp. acquires Datron Systems Inc.)," *San Diego Business Journal*, August 13, 2001. Also available at http://www.highbeam.com/DocPrint.aspx?DocId=1G1:77676308
3. Napoleonic Guide, "Napoleon on Politics and Power," http://www.napoleonguide.com/aquote_power.htm
4. Quotes and Poem.com, American First Lady Quotes, http://www.quotesandpoem.com/quotes/listquotes/author/rosalynn-carter
5. Legacee, "Leadership Definitions," Southern California, http://www.legacee.com/Info/Leadership/Definitions.html (accessed September 30, 2009).

6. Ken Blanchard, *Management of Organizational Behavior: Leading Human Resources, 8th ed.* (Upper Saddle River, NJ: Prentice Hall), 79.

7. Wall Street Journal Online, "Madoff Fraud Case," http://online.wsj.com/ public/page/bernard-madoff.html (accessed October 1, 2009).

8. Paul Tournier, *The Violence Within* (New York: HarperCollins, 1982), 151.

9. Reuters, "Bernard Madoff arrested over alleged $50 billion fraud," http:// www.reuters.com/article/topNews/idUSTRE4BA7IK20081212 (accessed October 2, 2009).

10. Bloomberg News, "Madoff to Forfeit $170 Billion In Assets Ahead of Sentencing," *The Washington Post*, June 27, 2009. Also available online at http://www.washingtonpost.com/wp-dyn/content/article/2009/06/26/ AR2009062604652.html

11. SourceWatch, "Enron Corporation," http://www.sourcewatch.org (accessed May 12, 2009).

12. Bill George, *True North: Discover Your Authentic Leadership* (San Francisco: Jossey-Bass, 2007), chaps. 1–2.

13. James M. Burns, *Transforming Leadership: The Pursuit of Happiness* (New York: Atlantic Monthly Press, 2003).

14. Answers.com, "redemption," http://www.answers.com/topic/redemption (accessed October 2, 2009).

15. Martin E.P. Seligman, *Learned Optimism: How to Change Your Mind and Your Life,* (New York: Pocket Books, 1990), chap. 1.

Chapter 2

1. Robert Browning, "A Death in the Desert." In *Dramatis Personae*, (London: Chapman and Hall, 1864).

2. John C. Maxwell, Ed. *Maxwell Leadership Bible: Revised and Updated: Briefcase Edition* (Nashville, TN: Thomas Nelson, 2008).

3. *The Wall*, Pink Floyd, 1979.

4. Rudolph W. Giuliani with Ken Kurson, *Leadership* (New York: Hyperion Books 2002), chap. 1.

Endnotes

5. Listverse, "7 Children Who Changed the World," 2008, http://listverse. com

6. James M. Kouzes and Barry Z. Posner, *The Leadership Challenge: The Most Trusted Source on Becoming a Better Leader,* 4th ed. (San Francisco: Jossey-Bass, 2008), 292.

Chapter 3

1. H. W. Crocker III, *Robert E. Lee on leadership: Executive lessons in character, courage, and vision* (Roseville, CA: Prima Lifestyles, 1999).

2. Fehrenbacher, ed., *Abraham Lincoln: Speeches and Writings 1859–1865: Speeches, Letters, and Miscellaneous Writings, Presidential Messages and Proclamations* (New York: Library of America, 2009).

3. Lockheed Martin, http://www.lockheedmartin.com/aboutus/index.html (accessed September 30, 2009).

4. *Securities and Exchange Commission v. The Titan Corporation*, 05-0411 (March 1, 2005), 2.

5. Securities and Exchange Commission, *Litigation Release No. 19107, Accounting and Auditing Enforcement Release No. 2204* (March 1, 2005).

6. Art Barter, interviewed by author, Vista, CA, May and June 2009.

7. Securities and Exchange Commission, *Form 10-K, 2004 Annual Report of The Titan Corporation* (Washington, D.C., 2005), 9. Also available online at http://www.sec.gov/Archives/edgar/data/32258/000104746905006804/ a2153658z10-k.htm.

8. David Rhodes and Daniel Stelter, "Seize Advantage in a Downturn." *Harvard Business Review,* February 2009.

9. Art Barter, interview by Business Performance Management, "*When Trust is King,*" June 4, 2009. Also available online at http://bpmmag.net/case_ studies/art-barter-datron-world-trust-0301/

10. ibid.

11. Liz Murray, speech at John Maxwell's Maximum Impact Simulcast, Dayton, OH, May 8, 2009. Text available at http://www.giantimpact.com/ dl/aftertheevent/mis09/mis09_lizmurray.pdf

Endnotes

Chapter 4

1. Ian Worthington, *Alexander the Great: Man and God* (Upper Saddle River, NJ: Longman, 2004).

2. American Psychiatric Association, *Diagnostic and Statistical Manual of Mental Disorders DSM-IV-TR Fourth Edition*, 4th ed. (Arlington, VA: American Psychiatric Publishing, Inc., 2000).

3. Augustine of Hippo, *The Confessions of St. Augustine: The Modern English Version* (Grand Rapids, MI: Revell, 2008), 165.

4. John C. Maxwell, *Leadership Gold: Lessons I've Learned from a Lifetime of Leading* (Nashville, TN: Thomas Nelson, 2008), 13.

5. Peter Senge, *The Fifth Discipline Fieldbook: The Art and Practice of the Learning Organization* (New York: Doubleday, 1994), 193–232.

6. Bill Hybels, *Courageous Leadership* (Grand Rapids, MI: Zondervan, 2009), chap. 11.

7. Steven R. Covey, *The Seven Habits of Highly Effective People* (New York: Fireside, 1990), chap. 1.

8. Howard Schultz, *Pour Your Heart Into It* (New York: Hyperion, 1999), 74.

9. Jack Welch, *Jack: Straight from the Gut* (New York: Warner Business Books, 2001), 3.

10. Benjamin Franklin, *The Autobiography of Benjamin Franklin* (Boston: Digireads, 2005), chap 8.

11. Daniel Trotta, "New York embraces hero pilot," *Reuters*, January 16, 2009. Also available at http://www.reuters.com/article/topNews/idUSTRE50E8AI20090117.

12. Quotations Book, "A little bit about Emerson, Ralph Waldo," http://quotationsbook.com/quote/10741/ (accessed October 2, 2009).

13. Finest Quotes, "Jim Ryun," http://www.finestquotes.com/author_quotes-author-Jim%20Ryun-page-0.htm (accessed October 2, 2009).

14. Stephen R. Covey, *The Seven Habits of Highly Effective People* (New York: Fireside, 1990), 46.

Endnotes

Chapter 5

1. Milton Friedman, "The social responsibility of business is to increase its profits," *The New York Times Magazine,* September 13, 1970. Copyright 1970 by The New York Times Company.
2. Ray Bradbury, *Reader's Digest,* January 1994.
3. CNN Money, Fortune, "World's Most Admired Companies, Top 50" http://money.cnn.com/magazines/fortune/mostadmired/2009/full_list/ (accessed October 1, 2009).
4. *American Compensation Journal,* Winter, 1995.
5. Southwest Airlines, "2008 Southwest Cares Report," 16. Available online at http://www.southwest.com/about_swa/southwest_cares/southwestcares _6_8_09.pdf
6. Jim Dowling, interview by author, Vista, CA, July 29, 2009.
7. ibid.
8. ibid.
9. The Quotations Page, Quotations by Author, "Steve Jobs," http://www.quotationspage.com/quotes/Steve_Jobs/ (accessed October 1, 2009).
10. John C. Maxwell, *Developing the Leaders Around You: How to Help Others Reach Their Full Potential* (Nashville, TN: Thomas Nelson, 2005), 11.
11. Malcolm Gladwell, *The Tipping Point: How Little Things Can Make a Big Difference* (New York: Little, Brown, and Company, 2000).
12. Linda Kaplan and Robin Koval, *The Power of Small: Why Little Things Make All the Difference* (New York: Broadway Business, 2009), chap. 1.
13. Gary Looper and Ann McGee-Cooper, *The Essentials of Servant-Leadership: Principles in Practice* (Waltham, MA: Pegasus Communications, Inc., 2001), chaps. 1–2.
14. Servant Leadership Institute, *Servant Leadership Level 1* (San Diego: L&L Digital Printers, 2009).
15. Servant Leadership Institute, *Servant Leadership Level 2* (San Diego: L&L Digital Printers, 2009).

Endnotes

Chapter 6

1. Clotaire Rapaille, *The Culture Code: An Ingenious Way to Understand Why People Around the World Live and Buy as They Do* (New York: Broadway Books, 2006), chap 1.

2. Society for Human Resources Management (SHRM), "2009 Employee Job Satisfaction, Executive Summary: Has the U.S. Recession Affected Employee Job Satisfaction?" http://www.shrm.org/Research/SurveyFindings/Articles/Documents/09-0282_Job_Satis_SR_Exec_Sum.pdf (accessed October 1, 2009).

3. Clotaire Rapaille, *The Culture Code: An Ingenious Way to Understand Why People Around the World Live and Buy as They Do* (New York: Broadway Books, 2006), 124.

4. Tom W. Smith, "Job Satisfaction in the United States," National Opinion Research Center, University of Chicago, April 17, 2007.

5. John C. Maxwell, *The 21 Irrefutable Laws of Leadership: Follow Them and People Will Follow You* (Nashville, TN: Thomas Nelson, 2007), chap. 1.

6. Douglas Hyde, *Dedication and Leadership: Learning from the Communists* (Notre Dame, IN: University of Notre Dame Press, 1966).

7. Martin Luther King, Jr., *The Autobiography of Martin Luther King, Jr.* (New York: Grand Central Publishing, 2001), 114, 187.

8. Britannica Encyclopedia Online, "Weather modification," http://www.britannica.com/EBchecked/topic/638346/weather-modification (accessed October 1, 2009).

9. National Center on Atmospheric Research (NCAR), "NCAR Online Education," http://ecourses.ncar.ucar.edu/ (accessed October 1, 2009).

10. Robert K. Greenleaf, *Servant Leadership: A Journey into the Nature of Legitimate Power & Greatness*, 25th ed. (Mahwah, NJ: Paulist Press, 2002), 27.

11. Mark Sattel, interviewed by author, Vista, CA, July 27, 2009.

12. Mark Sattel, electronic mail to author, Datron World Communications, Inc., July 27, 2009.

Endnotes

Chapter 7

1. *The Holy Bible, Authorized King James Version*, Proverbs 29:18.
2. Fortune 500 Mission Statements, http://www.missionstatements.com/fortune_500_mission_statements.html (accessed October 1, 2009).
3. Carol Malinski, interview with author, July 30, 2009.
4. ibid.
5. Stephen M. R. Covey, *The Speed of Trust: The One Thing That Changes Everything* (New York: Free Press, 2008), 30.
6. Plato, *The Republic* (New York: Penguin Classics, 2007), 392.
7. ibid.
8. Alexander Solzhenitsyn, Address at Harvard University, June 8, 1978. Available at http://www.columbia.edu/cu/augustine/arch/solzhenitsyn/harvard1978.html
9. Thomas Aquinas, *Summa Theologica, I-II, Qu.61, a.2* (Grand Rapids, MI: Christian Classics, 1981).
10. Plato, *The Republic* (New York: Penguin Classics, 2007), 43.
11. The Quotations Page, "Socrates," http://www.quotationspage.com/quotes/Socrates (accessed on October 2, 2009).

Chapter 8

1. The Gesundheit Institute, "History," http://www.patchadams.org/history_phases_I-V (accessed on October 1, 2009).
2. The Gesundheit Institute, "Global Outreach," http://www.patchadams.org/Gesundheit_Global_Outreach (accessed on October 1, 2009).
3. Fidelity Charitable Gift Fund 2008 Annual Report, "Inspiring the Future of Philanthropy," http://www.charitablegift.org/learn-about-charity/overview.shtml (accessed on October 1, 2009).
4. Datron World Communications, Inc. Charitable Fund Activity Summary.
5. Letty Edwards, interviewed by author, August 13, 2009.
6. Letty Edwards, electronic mail to author, Datron World Communications, Inc., August 13, 2009.
7. *The Holy Bible, New International Version*, Matthew 6:3–4.

Endnotes

8. Sheri Nasim, electronic mail to author, Datron World Communications, Inc., August 14, 2009.

9. Chronicle of Philanthropy, "Biden's Average Annual Charitable-Gift Total: $369," http://philanthropy.com/news/government/5685/bidens-average-annual-charitable-gift-total (accessed October 1, 2009).

10. Chronicle of Philanthropy, "Barack and Michelle Obama Donated $240,000 to Charity Last Year," http://philanthropy.com/news/updates/4219/barack-and-michelle-obama-donated (accessed October 1, 2009).

11. Chronicle of Philanthropy, "Gov. Palin Releases Tax Returns, Reveals Charitable Giving," http://philanthropy.com/news/updates/5900/gov-palin-releases-tax-returns-reveals (accessed October 1, 2009).

12. Chronicle of Philanthropy, "John McCain Discloses Data on His Charity Giving," http://philanthropy.com/news/updates/4437/mccain (accessed October 1, 2009).

13. Datron World Communications, Inc., Interoffice Memo, December 3, 2008. Subject: Datron World Communications Charitable Fund.

14. Douglas Pike, "Vietnam in 1991: The Turning Point," *Asian Survey*, Vol. 32, No. 1, *A Survey of Asia in 1991: Part I* (1992), 74–81.

15. Sarah Nguyen, interview with and electronic mail to author, Datron World Communications, Inc., August 14, 2009.

16. Free Wheelchair Mission, letter to Datron World Communications, Inc., January 22, 2009.

About the Author

Tony Baron is president of the Servant Leadership Institute of Datron World Communications, headquartered in Vista, California. He holds a double doctorate in psychology and theology and serves as adjunct professor in pastoral theology and leadership development at Fuller Theological Seminary and Azusa Pacific University.

Dr. Baron teaches, trains, and consults with corporate and church leaders around the world on how to live for the sake of others. He has authored four previous books. An ordained Anglican priest, Dr. Baron is board certified in forensic medicine, and he is a diplomate of the American Board of Psychological Specialties.

About Servant Leadership Institute

Building Servant Leaders to Transform Organizations

Servant Leadership Institute is a resource created to serve you and to help you build an organization that is determined to make a positive difference in the world. We not only link like-minded servant leaders with each other but we help them with strategic vision, training, and resources. Here are some ways SLI can serve you:

- Servant Leadership Summit—A once a year, two-and-a-half day conference to envision and equip servant leaders with greater leadership gifts and skills. Presented live in San Diego, this conference is designed to increase the leadership effectiveness of organization leaders worldwide. Two special modules on the various aspects of servant leadership are provided. They feature nationally known speakers in the corporate and church world.

- Servant Leadership Resources—Trusted and field-tested publications, training manuals, newsletters, and field guides that can be used by your trainers or serve as library resources within your corporation or church.

- Conference Speaking and Training Opportunities—Dr. Tony Baron, Datron owner Art Barter, and a talented array of servant leader speakers are available for your organization. Training classes can be provided to your organization as needed.

- Servant Leadership Consulting—Our team can provide long- or short-term mentoring for those interested in becoming a better servant leader. Our experienced team walks with you through the process of transformation.

Servant Leadership Institute is committed to serving you. If you are an organization with limited financial means, Datron World Communications is willing to provide scholarships so that your future servant leaders can be inspired, equipped, and encouraged to make a difference in the world.

For more specific information about Servant Leadership Institute, please call (760) 597-3796 or visit the website at www.forthesakeofothers. com.

CPSIA information can be obtained at www.ICGtesting.com
Printed in the USA
LVOW061924140312

273047LV00002B/6/P